HOW TO BREAK THROUGH BARRIERS AND ACHIEVE POWER RESULTS

CREATE YOUR POWER MINDSET FOR SUCCESS

IN 30 DAYS OR LESS

MADELINE ALEXANDER

THE POWER COACH™

Creative Communications Group International
Houston, TX

Published by Creative Communications Group International
P.O. Box 3109, #19275, Houston, TX 77253

Printed in the United States of America

Alexander, Madeline
How to Break through Barriers and Achieve Power Results, Create Your Power Mindset for Success in 30 Days or Less, by Madeline Alexander

ISBN 13: 978-1-936155-51-4
ISBN 10: 1-936155-51-6

DEDICATION

This book is dedicated to my precious mother, Alice R. Edwards. Mom, I love you dearly. Thank you for all of the sacrifices you made and challenges you endured to make my dreams possible. Thank you for staying the course and overcoming adversity against all odds. Thank you for carefully nurturing my self-esteem, and instilling in me the unwavering belief that I could accomplish anything that I set my mind to do. Thank you for teaching me that being a beautiful black woman is an extraordinary blessing to be carried with regal grace, noble character, and the utmost integrity. Thank you for everything, Mom. My blessings are your blessings; my success is your success.

To my brother and sisters – Rob Columbus, Jackie Edwards, and Eunice Young – thank you for always looking out for your baby sister and helping me with many of the experiences that ultimately have evolved into these concepts! To Allison, Josiah, Jack, Marc, John, Jonathan, Åse, and all of my extended family members, thank you for your love and support of your auntie, niece, and cousin. You are all special and important to me, and I love you.

To my Heavenly Father, I love you with all of my heart and my life is completely devoted to You. Through You, all things are possible to those who believe. Thank you for giving me the words to encourage, motivate, challenge, and inspire others to create an exceptional life worth living.

WHAT OTHERS ARE SAYING

"If you are ready to create your power mindset that leads you to awesome achievement, then read and use these simple, but powerful ideas from my friend Madeline Alexander! She is an amazing person with a huge heart who truly wants you to become UNSTOPPABLE!"

James Malinchak
Co-Author, Chicken Soup for the College Soul
"2-Time College Speaker of the Year!"
Founder, www.BigMoneySpeaker.com

"The reason this book is powerful enough to change your life is because it was written by someone who is already powerful, who streams her power-mind into power-principles for a life altering power-experience. Real power is generated in greatness. Whether you have met The Power Coach in person to feel that flow of power or you are reading these power tips to apply to your own life, Madeline Alexander is a conduit of power for you and to your life. Just being around her or reading her book makes me want to experience her same magnetic energy, power, and success. You will too! Madeline is a powerful enough light to light the path of your life."

Sandra L. Brown, M.A.
CEO of The Institute for Relational Harm Reduction, survivor services for those recovering from relationships with pathologically disordered partners. She is the author of 7 books including How to Spot a Dangerous Man and the award-winning Women Who Love Psychopaths. She is a therapist, author, and lecturer on women's issues and directs a large online magazine, www.saferelationshipsmagazine.com.

CONTENTS

ACKNOWLEDGMENTS

I would like to thank the following people who have made wonderful contributions to my life, and who make up the rich support system that has helped me to create Power Coaching™ and to complete this book.

To my business coach and mentor James Malinchak, thank you for getting me to absolute clarity, expanding my thinking, and sharing your extraordinary knowledge and experience! You are the BEST! I look forward to going to exponentially greater heights!

To my faithful friends - Joy Voith, Kamar Gore, Craig McFarlane, Karen Taylor, and Rosalyn Caldwell - thank you for your unwavering belief in me, daily encouragement, and unconditional support. I appreciate you being just a phone call away at all times!

To Pastors Marshall and Cindi Townsley, thank you for 22 years of faithful friendship and pastoral care. Marshall, you are truly the epitome of what a Pastor should be in every sense of the word. Thank you for always being there for me. Cindi, thank you for being such a phenomenal role model of a strong, powerful woman! You helped me to be true to myself! I appreciate you so much. We are joined for life!

To Sandra Brown, whose amazing work facilitated an essential breakthrough and who is helping me to assist many others with vital knowledge, my deepest thanks and gratitude!

To Latisha Bell and all of my extraordinary Power Coaching™ clients: your trust, transparency, and tenacity have allowed me to formulate this writing. Our conversations helped me immensely to pinpoint how to express these concepts clearly for a broader audience. Thank you!

To Avery Washington, thank you for your friendship and assistance with the details! It is rare for someone to extend themselves as you have done for me. I appreciate it greatly.

To my faithful readers of *Today's Power Tip for Success*, thank you for your notes, encouragements, and success stories! I always look forward to my interactions with you!

To my protégé' LaTorria Jones and your gracious family, thank you for your love and for allowing me to speak into your life. You are such a special treasure to me!

To my extended families at Lakewood Church, Houston, Texas; Champions Centre, Tacoma, Washington; and the Believers Center of Albuquerque, Albuquerque, New Mexico; thank you for being the bedrock of my life! You give me tremendous strength, joy, and encouragement!

To all of the special friends, co-workers, and business partners who have contributed to my life in different seasons and times, you may not be mentioned by name, but you are a big part of this story. Thank you.

INTRODUCTION

THIS BOOK IS FOR YOU

I am committed to your success! No matter where you are right now - living a good life, or struggling to make it - I want to help you to break through the barriers, and take your life to a whole new level. We all have the desire to climb higher, and to reach for greater things than what we are experiencing right now. I feel that desire, too. I am compelled by the drive in me to become the best person I can possibly be, and to help the people that truly want to be helped along the way. Many of the concepts you will read in this book I learned from my own trials and struggles, and the changes I had to undergo personally to overcome them. I had to go through the process of creating the Power Mindset for Success myself, even though I didn't know that was what was happening at the time. I realize now that many of the challenges I went through, and the phenomenal successes that I have experienced since then, have given me the depth of insight to share with you.

This is not a book of theories or academic concepts that have not been tried and tested. This is not a book by someone who is so far away from your life experiences that you cannot relate. I have been right where you are, and I have conquered the same challenges you are facing now. I have combined my personal life experiences with what I have learned from years of study, professional practice, and client validation to produce a real-life, no-nonsense guide to what it takes to produce the Power Mindset for Success. I am the Power Coach™. I have helped many people just like you to transform their minds, and get massive results they couldn't have imagined before we started to work together. This book is devoted to you - the climber, the overcomer, the conqueror, the fighter - who is tired of the status quo, and who is ready to break through the barriers that are holding you back, and produce the extraordinary life that you desire.

A Glimpse into My Story

I want to share a little bit of my story with you. I was talking to a Power Coaching™ member recently, and I was sharing with her how I had overcome a particular barrier she was currently facing. I was explaining the challenge and how I had beaten it. She was shocked! *"YOU went through this? I would have NEVER guessed that, EVER!"* You see, when you meet a successful, confident person, it's easy to assume they haven't been through what you might be dealing with. Trust me; I have overcome some things in my life, just like the issues you may be facing. Let me tell you a bit of my story that relates to the Power Mindset for Success.

For several years, I had a very successful career in corporate America, working for top Fortune 500 companies, including Microsoft Corporation, The Boeing Company, and Baxter International. I also had a successful stint working for the United States Air Force as a contract negotiator, which was a great position that I enjoyed very much. However, although I succeeded in the government and private sectors, I was always entrepreneurial at heart. While in the corporate environment, I always felt like I had my shoes on the wrong feet. I could walk, run, and jump through all the hoops, but it never felt right for me. It felt awkward, like my jacket was on too tight. I felt stifled and boxed in. Others around me loved the environment and absolutely thrived in the corporate sector, and I was very happy for them. Sometimes I even envied their comfort, ease, and flow. They seemed to be happy and clicking on all cylinders. I performed well, I was promoted, and I excelled, but on the inside, it just wasn't for me. I couldn't find my place. I was an entrepreneur trapped in a job.

In the mid-1990's, I stepped out to start my own business! I left my job at The Boeing Company. I had a great concept and message, but I didn't have the right mindset, mentor, or methods to build the business, and I failed. I was not prepared for the rigors of entrepreneurship, I didn't have the right system, and I didn't have the right coach to help me. I got off track in my approach and it cost me. I got away from my mission, core skills, and competencies. The supplier of a key component to my business decided to stop producing the product I needed, and just like that, the bottom fell out of my business plan. I didn't have a Plan B, and I didn't know how to adjust to get back to my core skillset. It was over. Just a year out of corporate, I had to go back to an 8-5 job. This was my first major failure in life.

I excelled through high school as a straight A student, accomplished musician, cheerleader, etc. I graduated magna cum laude from the University of Kansas with a Bachelor of Science degree in Business Administration, with several job offers waiting. I won numerous awards in each position I had held in corporate America. I was prospering and succeeding. I had a lot of friends and a rich social life. The business failure deeply impacted me, and I started to question myself. How did I end up going down the wrong road? Some of the closest people around me questioned me, too, which didn't help at all. I heard a lot of negative words and

Monday morning quarterbacking. *"I told you it wouldn't work. You should stick with what you can do. That was a dumb idea."*

Self-doubt is like an acid that eats away at whatever it comes in contact with. My failure fixation went beyond the business. My self-esteem was shaken, and I felt inferior for the first time in my life compared to other people. Listening to my internal and external critics, I started questioning everything – my intelligence, my drive, my beauty, my personality, my talents, and my abilities. I did not give up on my mission, but my self-confidence was in free-fall. I fell into the "someday" trap. Someday I would get back out there and try again. In the meantime, I poured myself into my new career at Microsoft. I tried to overcome my business failure with more corporate success. Externally, I was very successful, but internally, it didn't work. I was not doing what I was supposed to be doing. I was not fulfilling my mission. I worked more and served more. I was overeating and overworking to compensate, but nothing helped. I was still doing some public speaking and I dabbled in some writing because that was my passion, and I was successful. I was building up a nice following for my speaking services. The turning point came when a huge opportunity presented itself for me to create a series of products based on my messages, and I was not ready. I was not prepared to seize the moment. Another opportunity lost! I was extremely frustrated being stuck in my job, knowing I had a far greater gift on the inside that I wasn't using fully because I wasn't mentally tough enough to step out again. I wasn't prepared mentally and my skills weren't ready for prime time.

That was the final straw. I said to myself, *"THIS IS IT. Enough is enough. It's time to get back on track with my vision and mission. I can do this."* I knew I had to reprogram my thoughts for success. On a daily basis, I started reading books, listening to teaching CDs, and getting mentally in shape. I shook off the prior business failure and focused on the future. I developed a detailed vision, goals, and an action plan. I learned from my previous mistakes and incorporated that knowledge into my improved plan. I revamped my self-concept and got my confidence back, plus some! I went back to school at night to get prepared. For two grueling years, I went to school two nights a week while working 60 hours a week in my corporate position. I invested every weekend for two years into my homework assignments and required readings. I was determined to finish. I made a decision I would do whatever it took to succeed this time. Nothing would stop me! I took every speaking opportunity I could. I honed my message and wrote my business plan. I still had Doubters and Dream Killers around me, but I decided I would listen to me and not to them. I had to change some of my friends! I continued to develop my Power Mindset.

While on the job, I focused on doing my very best work as preparation for my business. I took on big projects that would stretch me and develop my skills, and I delivered. I racked up win after win for the company. I saved money for the transition. I moved across the country from Seattle, Washington to Houston, Texas to strategically locate my new company. I lost the extra weight I had gained – 30 pounds - and got my body into excellent physical condition to prepare for the challenges of entrepreneurship. I reevaluated my relationships and developed the right support system around me. I galvanized my will and determination to succeed. I summoned my courage, boldness, and bravery to tackle every challenge that presented itself. I invoked my endurance, perseverance, and tenacity to stay the course without wavering. I continued to rewrite my mental soundtrack to speak only of success. When I started my new business, I had a completely different mindset, skillset, and strategy. I was a completely different person physically, mentally, emotionally, and spiritually. On a scale of 1 to

10, my confidence level was at 17 and climbing! I felt, and continue to feel, ecstatic about myself, my life, and my future. I showed new resilience and agility, bouncing back from small setbacks and the unexpected, adjusting my plans as new information became available. This time, instead of operating on my own, I invested in the right coaches who could guide my process and progress. Success was inevitable and imminent. This time, I had the Power Mindset for Success!

I now have gone on to far greater successes in every area of my life professionally and personally. I not only have mastered this process for myself, but I have mastered how to share it very effectively with others. I created a revolutionary rapid results coaching system, Power Coaching™, that enables me to help others break through barriers, banish limiting beliefs, master success habits, and transform every area of their lives in the shortest possible period of time. I have helped many other people conquer similar challenges and go on to great success in their lives. Today, I will begin to do the same thing for you!

Why I Wrote This Book

I have dedicated my life to helping people break through barriers, and achieve power results fast. I am passionate about helping people get through all the junk – the fears, the limiting beliefs, self-sabotaging habits, and the faulty thinking - that is keeping them from achieving what they want. I love to roll up my sleeves and help my Power Coaching™ members get results quickly. Nothing fires me up more than helping someone get a major breakthrough in their thinking, or seeing a client put all the pieces together, get their momentum, and catapult themselves forward to a whole new level. I invented Power Coaching™ to help people transform their lives and produce power results rapidly. I show others how to create a strong business, elevate their career, super-charge their health, and develop deep, rewarding relationships. Given the strong results I had produced with Power Coaching™, I began writing what I thought would be the foundational book on my core principles of how to break through barriers, and achieve power results fast.

However, I realized that in order for you to use all that I want to share with you, you first have to get your mind in shape. You must have the right mental conditioning to use the power principles most effectively.

Athletes don't start competing until they have trained and conditioned their bodies to handle the demands of their sport. The same is true for success. So often, I encounter people who are frustrated with their attempts to succeed and the meager results they have produced, but they have not done the mental conditioning necessary to develop a mindset that will produce success and sustain them through the inevitable setbacks. If your mindset is flabby and out of shape, you are not going to be able to sustain the effort it takes to succeed. I could teach you all the success strategies you could ever need, but you will not use them to change if you don't have the mental toughness to stay the course and make it work. At the first sign of a challenge, the mental softness will defeat you, and you will be tempted to pull back, turn back, tuck tail, and give up. A professional athlete gets ready at the beginning of the season to endure the long road ahead. You and I must condition our minds for the challenge of elevating our lives to a new summit. You don't embark on the journey with no preparation!

You must have the courage, the focus, the fearlessness, the risk tolerance, the endurance, the strong self-concept, the confidence, the boldness, and many other qualities to get out there, take action, overcome obstacles, and make it happen. If you are soft mentally, you are going to get soft, insignificant results. If you are strong and powerful mentally, you are going to produce power results. No matter what happens to you externally, no matter what circumstances come, if you have the Power Mindset for Success, you have the internal will to succeed, and you are going to rise above what comes and lay hold of your success no matter what. You will not waver, whimper, cower, or cringe from anything. When you have the Power Mindset, you are not blown off course by problems, or shaken by circumstances. You are steadfast and immovable, ready to take on whatever comes your way.

In Phase 1 of Power Coaching™, I help my coaching members break through the barriers that are holding them back. After facilitating breakthrough after breakthrough, and by deeply evaluating my own successes and setbacks, I have identified several common areas of mental softness that need to be eliminated so you can get results quickly in every area of your life. To help my Power Coaching™ members, I began to write a short, daily motivational message to reinforce key concepts and the big wins they were experiencing. This is how *Today's Power Tip for Success* was born! (You are more than welcome to subscribe at **www.madelinealexander.com**). Each message describes an aspect of the Power Mindset. The response was overwhelming! Readers on my mailing list started sending *Today's Power Tip for Success* to their families, friends, and co-workers. Managers and leaders started sharing the messages with their teams. Entrepreneurs were using the Power Tips in sales meetings to motivate their employees and partners. I started getting thank you emails from all over the United States with people telling me they were getting breakthroughs just by reading *Today's Power Tip for Success*, and to please keep them coming. The Power Tips provided just the right boost to get them over the hump. I heard stories of new businesses being started after the business plans had sat dormant, new books being written, and brave, bold moves that were starting to take place. Projects that had been sitting on shelves were being dusted off, revamped, and revitalized. New ideas were taking shape. People were developing the courage to start. I wasn't sharing any of my tools or strategies yet! I was sharing (and I continue to share) vital concepts to change the way that the readers were thinking about themselves and their circumstances. I recognized that this work on developing the Power Mindset was an essential precursor to any other work or any other writing I would do.

I asked my coaching members, friends, and family, "Would you read a book that helped you first get your mindset in shape for success? Would you apply a program that focused on revving up your mental conditioning, so you developed the resolve to succeed?"

"YES!! HURRY UP," was the response! "WHAT ARE YOU WAITING FOR?" (That one made me laugh, as it is one of my trademark sayings that I use daily! It was funny to have it used back on me!) So I temporarily interrupted my writing of the power principles book to create the "prequel," a mental conditioning program that will first get your mind in shape and rock hard, ready to produce power results.

This Book is a Mental Conditioning Program

How to Break through Barriers and Achieve Power Results; Create Your Power Mindset for Success in 30 Days or Less is a mental conditioning program. It is a fitness program for the mind, and I am your personal trainer.

I am a no-nonsense, get-to-the-point type of person. I like to do stuff quickly. With my coaching members, I'm not going to take six months to tell them what I see in the first six minutes. We get right to it, starting in Session 1. I don't like programs that take forever to work. I like to know right away that I am getting somewhere! For example, I like fitness programs where I can feel something is happening in my body. I like to feel encouraged, motivated, and invigorated! I want this program to feel the same way for you. You can do this program easily in 30 days or less. Feel free to do it faster! You can get your mindset in shape quickly, and then apply what you have learned right away to produce power results in your life.

EASY INSTRUCTIONS

HOW TO USE THIS BOOK EFFECTIVELY

If you are an athlete, then you already know about "two-a-days." If not, let me introduce this phenomenal concept to you. The concept of two-a-days is that, for a short period of time, you do two conditioning sessions a day in order to double your conditioning time and produce massive results quickly. Athletes from all kinds of sports – football, basketball, baseball, bodybuilding, tennis, swimming, softball, track & field, etc. – professional, amateur, and high school athletes alike – use two-a-days in their training regimens when their goal is to focus and get in shape fast. Two-a-days are commonly part of pre-season preparations, and also can be used for fast tune-ups before the play-offs or major competitions and championships. In high school, being more of the creative type, I even used two-a-days as a musician to get prepared for big concerts and competitions! I have a friend that used two-a-days to go to Alcoholics Anonymous meetings to beat an alcohol addiction! Two-a-days can work for anything if you have the right program!

One of the principles of excellent mental conditioning is to read something that feeds your mind first thing in the morning and right before going to bed at night. Aha! Two-a-days! I have designed my mental conditioning program in the two-a-day format.

I'm asking you to use an easy program of two-a-days lasting just 15 minutes each for 30 days. That's it! Will you set aside 15 minutes each morning and 15 minutes at night before you go to bed to radically change your thinking and create your Power Mindset for Success? Don't even start with the "I don't have time" excuse. That is a barrier to your success. We all are given 24 hours a day, and it is up to you to steward your time wisely so that you are getting maximum results. If you take the time you would spend on a 30 minute television show, a chit-chat phone call, or your daily web surfing, you can INVEST that time into transforming your life. So, set up your morning so that you have 15 minutes to devote to your success. I recommend you do this right after you take time to pray and be thankful for all of the blessings in your life. Give thanks and get focused on what is important.

Your 15 minutes in the morning will be structured like this:

1. Read the Power Tip. For the slowest reader on the planet, this will take no more than five minutes!
2. Think about how the Power Tip applies to your life and what you need to do to elevate your thinking. Jot down a few thoughts to capture your insights.
3. Write down one action you will take to apply the Power Tip in the next 24 hours. You are done!

At night you will do the same thing. For 15 minutes in the evening right before you go to bed, read the Power Tip, apply it to yourself, and write down one action you can take in the next 24 hours to anchor it into your thinking. That's it! Easy!

If you want to read ahead and do the program faster, do it! In 30 days or less, you will have mentally conditioned your mind for success. You will have burned off the fat of faulty thinking and limiting beliefs, pumped up your passion and purpose, firmed up your fighting machines of endurance, perseverance and tenacity, pressed through fear and unbelief, and you will be flexing the sleek, strong muscles of the Power Mindset for Success 30 days from today. So get your warm-ups on and let's get started!

Fill in your name below:

I, ______________________________, am ready to create My Power Mindset for Success. I am ready to banish my fears, faulty thinking, and limiting beliefs. I will fortify my will and develop the determination necessary to accomplish my goals. I will mentally condition my mind for success in 30 days or less. I will invest 15 minutes each morning and 15 minutes every night to radically transform my thoughts, and take my life to a whole new level.

____

Your Signature

DAY 1 | A.M.

DECLARE YOUR INDEPENDENCE

"Once in awhile it really hits people that they don't have to experience the world in the way they have been told to."

–Alan Keightley

The ability to think independently, breaking away from the conventional wisdom of the crowd, resisting peer pressure, and giving yourself permission to step out of the status quo, will enable you to design the life of your dreams. To unlock the untapped and unrealized potential inside of you, you must first allow yourself to envision an extraordinary life, and then indisputably believe that you can and will design, create, and manifest the life you see. You can choose to allow the culture to dictate to you what your world can be, or you can choose to listen to the voice of purpose within you. You can listen to the dominant thinking of society, or you can choose to see the potential of your world with eyes of faith. It is your choice. You can fill your mind with negative news reports and startling statistics, or you can train your mind to be an engine of ideas, an incubator of innovation, and a wellspring of wealth and wisdom. You can choose to progress and prosper, or retreat and recede. You can be fearless or fearful. It is up to you. You can choose to be generous in a world of greed and selfishness. You can succeed being caring and compassionate, not cut-throat and callous. The choices are set before you. What you choose to think and believe will define what you achieve. Choose your own way. Determine to rise higher. Declare your independence!

Power Principle

Don't copy the behavior and customs of this world, but let God transform you into a new person by changing the way you think. Then you will learn to know God's will for you, which is good and pleasing and perfect.

Romans 12:2 (NLT)

Power Thoughts

Action Step

DAY 1 | P.M.

STAND UP, STAND OUT, AND STAND STRONG!

"To go against the dominant thinking of your friends, of most of the people you see every day, is perhaps the most difficult act of heroism you can have."

–Theodore White

Are you purpose-driven or peer-driven? To experience extraordinary success, you cannot think and act like everyone around you. You must have the courage to make your own choices and decisions that align with your destiny. You must be willing to step out of the pack, disagree, dissent, and deviate from the prevalent thinking of the crowd. Group thinking will imprison your possibilities in the penitentiary of peer pressure. Your individuality is on lock-down; your creativity is confined. Your purpose is imprisoned; your destiny detained. Do you make decisions based on what everyone else is doing? Are you a prisoner to the opinions of others? Do you seek validation from your peer group before embracing your own ideas and concepts? Are you jailed by peer group judgments? Shake off the shackles of sameness! Break out of bondage and be true to yourself! Do you have the courage to live your values in spite of the morality of the masses, or do you crumble when questioned? Are you listening to the crowd or your Creator? Free your future from the grip of group thinking. Free yourself from being a follower. Free yourself from the prison of peer pressure. Stand up, stand out, and stand strong!

Power Principle

Saul gave in and confessed, “I’ve sinned. I’ve trampled roughshod over GOD’s Word and your instructions. I cared more about pleasing the people. I let them tell me what to do.”

1 Samuel 15:24 (The Message)

Power Thoughts

Action Step

DAY 2 | A.M.

DO YOU SEE WHAT I SEE?

"I only wish you could see what I see when I look at you."
-Kobi Yamada

When you look in the mirror, what do you see? Do you see the common, the ordinary, or the extraordinary? Do you see your past or your potential? Do you see failure or the fantastic finish destined in your future? Do you see the trials or the triumph? Do you see mediocrity or magnificence? It is time for you to see yourself as the unique and truly amazing person that you are. It is time to redefine your self-perception to accurately reflect the perspective of your Creator, who made you in the image of greatness. It is time to shed your self-criticism, and hyper-focus on past mistakes and failures. Are you beating yourself up, or building yourself up? Now is the time to celebrate the extraordinary in you. I see you through the eyes of the One that made you for this time and for a purpose. I see power, strength, and beauty. I see integrity, honesty, and loyalty. I see endurance, tenacity, and perseverance. I see a creative genius. I see a leader. I see a brilliant business owner; an extraordinary entrepreneur. I see a loving, nurturing mother, and a committed, compassionate father. I see kindness, generosity, and compassion. I see determination, diligence, and destiny. I see a conqueror, an overcomer, and world changer. Do you see what I see?

Yet in all these things we are more than conquerors through Him who loved us.

Romans 8:37 (NKJV)

Day 2 | P.M.

EQUIPPED TO BE EXTRAORDINARY

"We all have the extraordinary coded within us, waiting to be released."
–J.L. Houston

At some point in your journey of achievement, you must come to fully realize who you are, and you must recognize the exceptional gifting that you carry within you. It does not serve you to play small and insignificant. Your brilliance was never intended to be bound and bridled. You were not created for containment. To be average is alien to your DNA. The compelling vision that burns within you is not by accident. The mission was not misplaced when it was placed in you. No, it was planned with precision, and entrusted to you on purpose, along with every gift and ability you will ever need to masterfully fulfill it. Your burning desire to rise higher and to break free of ritual and routine is the extraordinary gifting inside of you demanding to be expressed. Will you release it? Will you silence the limiting beliefs that question your qualifications? Will you shake off the self-criticism that scrutinizes your skills? Don't miss your moment by tearing down your talents!

There is no need to second-guess yourself. You have everything you need to succeed! Stop underestimating your excellence! You are thoroughly equipped for every great work. You are encoded with the exceptional. You are equipped to excel. You are empowered to exceed all expectations. You are equipped to be extraordinary!

Power Principle

For we are God's masterpiece. He has created us anew in Christ Jesus, so we can do the good things he planned for us long ago.

Ephesians 2:10 (NLT)

Power Thoughts

Action Step

DAY 3 | A.M.

YOUR VISION IS YOUR VICTORY

"There is no passion to be found playing small – in settling for a life that is less than the one you are capable of living."

–Nelson Mandela

What is your vision? Do you have a vision for your life that expands far beyond your present reality, and demands the development of your abilities and aptitudes? Or, have you acquiesced to average; succumbed to the status quo? Have you quietly accepted that what you have right now, and what you have accomplished to date is all there is for you? Decide now you will not settle where you are! There is far more in you than what you see right now. You have a rich reservoir of resources stored up within you. Place a demand on your potential by challenging yourself to see what can be. What stirs your passion? What do you love to do? What can you create? If you allowed yourself to use your highest intellect, your secret skills, your treasured talents, and your captive creativity, what would happen? What if you unlocked your abilities and unleashed your personal power? What problem could you solve for the world? What could you invent?

Who could you help? What suffering could you silence? Developing a compelling vision for your life is the key to your future happiness, fulfillment, and prosperity. Steve Jobs, CEO of Apple, said, "If you are working on something exciting that you really care about, you don't have to be pushed. The vision pulls you." Let a new vision pull you forward. Your vision is your victory!

Power Principle

Now Jabez was more honorable than his brothers…And Jabez called on the God of Israel saying, "Oh, that You would bless me indeed, and enlarge my territory, that Your hand would be with me, and that You would keep me from evil, that I may not cause pain!" So God granted him what he requested.

1 Chronicles 4:9-10 (NKJV)

Power Thoughts

Action Step

DAY 3 | P.M.

WHAT DID YOU COME HERE FOR?

"I didn't come here to be average."
–Michael Jordan

What did you come here for? Did you show up to be silent or spectacular? Mediocre or magnificent? Standard or stunning? Think about why you started your small business, accepted the promotion, or created your company. What did you envision when you got married, became a parent, launched your ministry, or committed to your cause? What goals did you set at the outset? What vision did you formulate in your mind? Did you set out to be average or outrageously successful? Les Brown put it this way: "No one rises to low expectations." It's time to raise your standards! Set a new standard for personal excellence. Choose to go beyond the usual and the common. What are you willing to accept from yourself? Do you excuse a lack of effort, excellence, or commitment? Define what is acceptable, and accept nothing less. Are you normal or a knockout? Tear down the typical, and take hold of being a trailblazer. Set your outlook to outstanding, your mindset to magnanimous! Make average unacceptable. Do not surrender to sameness. Greatness is within your grasp! It's time to seize your success. The choice is yours. Will you muddle in mediocrity or make your mark? What did you come here for?

Power Principle

Do you see a man diligent and skillful in his business? He will stand before kings; he will not stand before obscure men.

Proverbs 22:29 (AMP)

Power Thoughts

Action Step

DAY 4 | A.M.

GOT GOALS?

"In the absence of clearly-defined goals, we become strangely loyal to performing daily trivia until ultimately we become enslaved by it."

–Robert Heinlein

Have you written a set of clearly defined goals? Are you driving toward your dream, or toiling in trivia? Several well documented studies have confirmed that only 10 percent of the population have specific, well-defined goals. 23 percent have no idea what they want from life, while 67 percent have a general idea of what they want, but they do not have any specific plans for how to get there. That means 90 percent of the people around you are drifting through life. Decide to take your mission seriously. This is not a dress rehearsal. This is show time. Are you headed for the Targeted 10% or the No-direction 90%? Take time to write out your vision in detail. Write down your specific goals, and create an action plan. You will sabotage your own success by not investing the time to clarify your direction and write it down. Your creative power will be released when you write. Your ability to incubate ideas and cultivate your vision will be unlocked when you set your plans to paper. It is your choice whether you will be mission-minded or trapped in daily trivia. Get goals to get going! The quality of your life in the years to come will be determined by the goals you are pursuing today. Got goals?

Power Principle

Then the LORD answered me and said: "Write the vision and make it plain on tablets, that he may run who reads it."

Habakkuk 2:2 (NKJV)

DAY 4 | P.M.

TRY SOMETHING!

"Above all, try something."
–Franklin D. Roosevelt

The search for the perfect answer can bring your progress to a grinding halt. Do not get paralyzed obsessively weighing your options. There will always be pros and cons to every action. Weigh your options, assess the benefits and risks, select the best option available, and move forward. If you do not get the results you want, make adjustments. You will get a lot farther in life taking action and making adjustments along the way, rather than taking no action in the fantasy search for the perfect solution. Above all, try something!

Power Principle

We humans keep brainstorming options and plans, but GOD's purpose prevails.

Proverbs 19:21 (The Message)

Power Thoughts

Action Step

DAY 5 | A.M.

STEAL SECOND!

"Progress always involves risks. You can't steal second and keep your foot on first."

–Frederick Wilcox

Increasing your tolerance for calculated risk will open a new world of opportunity for you. Get acquainted with the sensations of stretching, striving, believing, and daring. Allow yourself to ponder new possibilities. Challenge yourself to expand your thinking. Will it feel uncomfortable? Initially, yes. Over time, you will get accustomed to the rigors of risk-taking. The craving for the familiar ease of the comfort zone will keep you on the outside of your destiny. You cannot fulfill a challenging goal or meaningful mission without acclimating yourself to the presence of risk. There are times when you will need to push yourself beyond safety and security. You cannot always hold onto what is familiar and predictable. When you raise your tolerance for risk, you greatly increase your opportunity for reward. Replace comfort with courage. Step out. Step forward. Stretch yourself. Steal second!

Power Principle

"Lord, if it's you," Peter replied, "tell me to come to you on the water." "Come," he said. Then Peter got down out of the boat, walked on the water and came toward Jesus. But when he saw the wind, he was afraid and, beginning to sink, cried out, "Lord, save me!" Immediately Jesus reached out his hand and caught him. "You of little faith," he said, "why did you doubt?"

Matthew 14:28-31 (NIV)

Power Thoughts

Action Step

Day 5 | P.M.

MAKE A BOLD MOVE!

"One cannot leap a chasm in two jumps."
–Winston Churchill

In your journey to success, you will encounter certain crossroads that will test your resolve to go forward. You must make a bold move forward or turn back empty-handed. There is no bridge to bolster you, or conduit to catch you. You will need to make a bold leap of faith. I remember when I moved across the country from Seattle, Washington to Houston, Texas to lay the groundwork to start my company. I had many chasms to cross. I was committed to building my own business, but I was leaving my professional and personal support systems to move to a city in which I had never lived and knew no one. I only knew my business would thrive if I would take the leap of faith. I was going to either make a bold move, or turn back to my comfort zone, where I was known, loved, and supported. I made a bold move. I remember counting down the days to the date I had set on the calendar to resign from my corporate position. I received a long overdue promotion just 30 days before my planned end date. I could enjoy the new perks and status, or stay true to my vision, leave the comfort of corporate America, and create my destiny. Staying could offer nothing but stagnation. I had to take the leap of faith, and embrace my freedom and future. I made a bold move, leaping forward into the unknown and unseen, to lay hold of my destiny. Are you encountering a crossroads today? Are you facing a chasm of change? I am standing on the other side, where destiny, mission, and vision reside, encouraging you to take your leap! Make a bold move!

Power Principle

GOD told Abram: "Leave your country, your family, and your father's home for a land that I will show you. I'll make you a great nation and bless you. I'll make you famous; you'll be a blessing. I'll bless those who bless you; those who curse you I'll curse. All the families of the Earth will be blessed through you."

Genesis 12:1-3 (The Message)

Power Thoughts

Action Step

DAY 6 | A.M.

MAKE THE DECISION TO FINISH

"Never give up, for that is just the place and time that the tide will turn."
–Harriet Beecher Stowe

There is one decision you do not revisit: the decision to finish. Making an iron-clad decision at the outset to finish your course will galvanize your determination, courage, and inner strength into a formidable force that will sustain you and propel you forward, even as you face the most difficult and seemingly insurmountable circumstances. Wavering weakens your will. Being steadfast and immovable in your decision to go the distance will sustain you through adversity. There is a point in every journey when your resolve to finish will be seriously tested. Your decision will be tested when you are tired, fatigued, or in pain. Your decision will be tested when it seems you do not have the resources to move forward. Your decision will be tested when you feel you are standing alone. Your decision will be tested when your methods aren't working, your ideas are rejected, and your proposals are turned down. Your decision will be tested when absolutely nothing seems to be happening. If you rehearse your decision every day to finish and not quit, to stay the course, and go the distance, you will be mentally prepared, emotionally grounded, and spiritually armored to pass the test when it arises. When you arrive at the turning point, the irreversible decision you made at the outset to finish your course will defy all odds, defeat your opponent, and drive you on to victory. The tide of the battle will turn. You will find a way. You will overcome. You will stand at the summit. You will fulfill your dream. Make the decision to go the distance, and you will live your destiny!

So let's not get tired of doing what is good. At just the right time we will reap a harvest of blessing if we don't give up.

Galatians 6:9 (NLT)

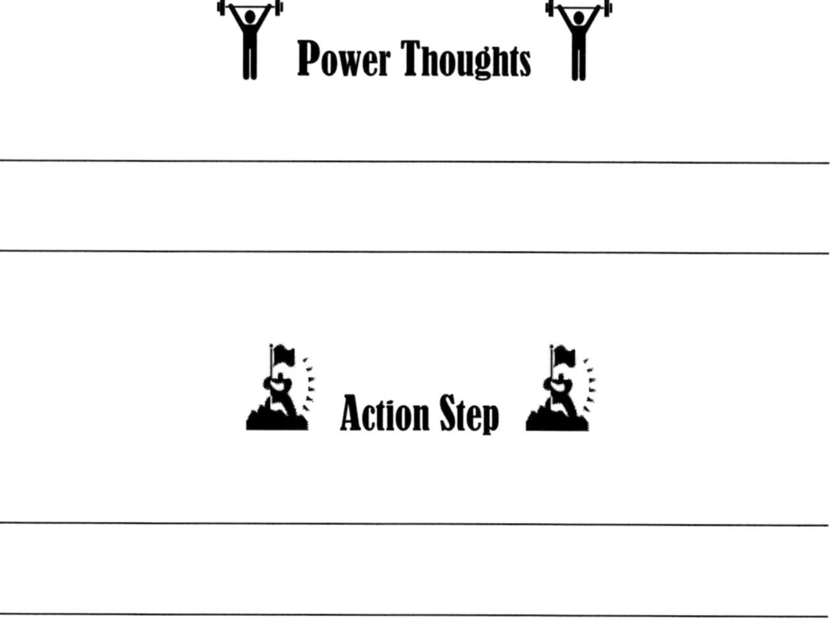

DAY 6 | P.M.

IGNITE YOUR REVOLUTION

"Always bear in mind that your own resolution to succeed is more important than any other one thing."

-Abraham Lincoln

More important than education, credentials, financial resources, connections, or even opportunity, is your personal resolve and unwavering commitment to succeed. When you decide once and for all, that you will fulfill the dream in your heart, that you will move forward no matter what comes, and that there is no turning back, you will ignite a great fire of passion within you. When there is no other option but to succeed, your relentless determination will incinerate all obstacles that rise in your path. You will find the answers to unanswerable questions, you will find abundant resources in the face of insufficiency, you will connect with the right coaches, mentors, and advisors to help you when you thought you were standing alone, and you will develop skills and abilities you had no idea that you had lying dormant inside. Your own immovable, unshakable, steadfast determination will cause your goals to manifest. Decide today, once and for all, you are going forward and you will not turn back. Your resolution will ignite your revolution!

Power Principle

Therefore, my beloved brethren, be steadfast, immovable, always abounding in the work of the Lord, knowing that your labor is not in vain in the Lord.

1 Corinthians 15:58 (NKJV)

Power Thoughts

Action Step

DAY 7 | A.M.

DESTROY ALL DOUBT

"A person who doubts himself is like a man who would enlist in the ranks of his enemies and bear arms against himself."

-Alexandre Dumas

Self-doubt is an insidious foe that you must conquer to achieve your vision. In the stillness, when you are alone with only your thoughts, do you feel dread, anxiety, and uneasiness, or a quiet, commanding confidence? When you close your eyes, do you see in detail the culmination of your hard work, perseverance, and determination? Stop and listen to your own inner thoughts. What are you saying to yourself? Do you hear, *"This will never work. I am not going to make it."* To overcome self-doubt and develop an unwavering belief in your dream, rewrite your internal script to forcefully speak to yourself with words that destroy all doubt. *"I am fully convinced that I will succeed. I am well able to fulfill my vision, goals, and dreams. I have everything I need to succeed, beginning today. I am extraordinarily talented, and gifted for greatness. I am creative, innovative, and I solve hard problems. The solutions to my challenges are well within my reach. My burning passion to overcome incinerates all obstacles in my path. I am disciplined, diligent, and driven to rise higher. I am tenacious and steadfast. I will never quit, give up, or turn back. I am strong and very courageous. I persevere through tough challenges. I see the finish line with my eyes of faith. I am more than a conqueror. I will live an exceptional life. I believe in myself."* Declare your victory and destroy all doubt!

For assuredly, I say to you, whoever says to this mountain, 'Be removed and be cast into the sea,' and does not doubt in his heart, but believes that those things he says will be done, he will have whatever he says.

Mark 11:23 (NKJV)

DAY 7 | P.M.

GUN 'EM DOWN!

"Whenever a negative thought concerning your personal power comes to mind, deliberately voice a positive thought to cancel it out."

–Norman Vincent Peale

As you mold your mindset for success, negative thoughts will still attempt to invade the airspace of your mind. These thoughts may spring up from negative statements others have said about you in the past. *("You'll never amount to anything. You'll never make it.")* They may pop up from your own lack of confidence. *("I'm not sure I can do this.")* Or they may come from the external circumstances that surround you. *("Small business failures are at an all-time high. Financial pressures push the divorce rate higher.")* You must be prepared with a strong strategy to take out these invaders at the first blip on your mental radar screen. When you see self-doubt and lack of confidence entering your airspace, it's time to take immediate action. It's time to lock and load. Don't allow these assailants to ambush your vision. Gun 'em down! When you detect limiting beliefs lurking on the horizon, gun 'em down! You must be ready with positive counter-statements that can immediately counteract the intruder's impact. When fears make a flagrant attack on your goals, gun 'em down! You have to constantly and vigilantly patrol and protect the airspace of your mind. When negative circumstances make a move on your mission, gun 'em down! Are you ready for the dogfight to protect your dream? You are the Top Gun responsible for your goals. No one else can fight this fight of faith for you. Be ready to cancel all negative thoughts. Blast those bandits! Gun 'em down!

Power Principle

For though we live in the world, we do not wage war as the world does. The weapons we fight with are not the weapons of the world. On the contrary, they have divine power to demolish strongholds. We demolish arguments and every pretension that sets itself up against the knowledge of God, and we take captive every thought to make it obedient to Christ.

2 Corinthians 10:3-5 (NIV)

Power Thoughts

Action Step

DAY 8 | A.M.

FACE YOUR FEAR

"I learned that courage was not the absence of fear, but the triumph over it. The brave man is not he who does not feel afraid, but he who conquers that fear."

–Nelson Mandela

As you rise to take hold of your vision, at some point, you will experience fear. It's a natural response to taking on a challenge, and moving forward into the unknown. What do you fear? Are you afraid you will fail? Do you fear rejection or ridicule? Are you afraid of what success may bring? Unknown and unnamed fear can paralyze you. Its unchallenged presence can shut down your will to move forward. Do not be held hostage by your fear. To succeed, you will need to face your fear! Do not pull back; look at it head-on. Confront it, name it, and disarm it. Ask yourself, *"What am I afraid of? What is the worst that can happen?"* Knowing that you have made a firm decision to finish, what will you do if what you fear comes to pass? By asking these questions, you will disarm the fear. Walk through it in your mind. See yourself conquering the situation. Now ask yourself,

"What is the best that can happen?" See yourself victorious in the face of challenges. Visualize yourself rising above the negative circumstance. Call forth your courage to move past your fear. Rehearse your victory in advance. You are well able to overcome any challenge. Boldness breaks through the barrier of fear. Be strong and courageous. Step forward. Face your fear!

THE LORD is my Light and my Salvation--whom shall I fear or dread? The Lord is the Refuge and Stronghold of my life--of whom shall I be afraid?

Psalm 27:1 (AMP)

DAY 8 | P.M.

DARE TO BE POWERFUL

"When I dare to be powerful, to use my strength in the service of my vision, then it becomes less and less important whether I am afraid."

–Audre Lord

Will you dare to be powerful? Courage is the ability to move forward and take action, even in the face of fear. Courage overrides fear; it does not wait for the fear to subside. As you pursue your vision, you will be faced with times when you must summon your personal power, conviction, faith, and inner strength to overcome the fear of failure, the fear of rejection, the fear of ridicule, and even the fear of success. I dare you to step forward today. Courage conquers all fears. Be strong and very courageous! Dare to be powerful!

Power Principle

Fear not [there is nothing to fear], for I am with you; do not look around you in terror and be dismayed, for I am your God. I will strengthen and harden you to difficulties, yes, I will help you; yes, I will hold you up and retain you with My [victorious] right hand of rightness and justice.

Isaiah 41:10 (AMP)

Power Thoughts

Action Step

DAY 9 | A.M.

WHAT IS YOUR FOCUS?

"Concentrate all your thoughts upon the work at hand. The sun's rays do not burn until brought to a focus."

–Alexander Graham Bell

Your power of focus – your ability to concentrate all of your attention, creativity, and action toward a chosen goal to the exclusion of other, lesser important things that are competing for your time and attention – will ultimately determine your level of achievement. What is distracting you from your primary goal? Narrow your focus. Tiger Woods, the legendary PGA golfer, is known for his extraordinary mental toughness, that allows him to focus while competing to the exclusion of all else, especially when he is under pressure, and a major championship is on the line. His focus? To win... period. What is your focus?

Power Principle

I want you woven into a tapestry of love, in touch with everything there is to know of God. Then you will have minds confident and at rest, focused on Christ, God's great mystery.

Colossians 2:2 (The Message)

Power Thoughts

____

____

____

Action Step

____

____

DAY 9 | P.M.

CHANGE YOUR PERSPECTIVE

"The trick is in what one emphasizes.
We either make ourselves miserable,
or we make ourselves happy.
The amount of work is the same."

–Carlos Castaneda

What are you focusing on? Every day, you will be presented with a combination of positive experiences, special opportunities for connection, magical moments, frustrations, irritants, challenges, and disappointments. Which will you focus on? Will you embrace and celebrate the good that is happening in your life, or will you fixate on the negative occurrences? The choice you make will determine how you experience your world, for the day, the week, the month, or the year. Your choice will determine whether you live today in joy, thankfulness, appreciation, and power, or anger, frustration, stress, and anxiety. It is solely your choice. It is not what happens to you that determines your reality. It is what you choose to focus on and magnify that will design your day. Do not fall prey to the disappointments and frustrations that come to devour your emotional strength. Put your energy, focus, emotion, and action toward the positive experiences and blessings in your life. Choose to make this and every day a phenomenal day of victory! Change your perspective!

Power Principle

Finally, brothers, whatever is true, whatever is noble, whatever is right, whatever is pure, whatever is lovely, whatever is admirable—if anything is excellent or praiseworthy—think about such things.

Philippians 4:8 (NIV)

Power Thoughts

Action Step

DAY 10 | A.M.

YOUR TIME IS COMING!

"To every person there comes that moment when he is figuratively tapped on the shoulder to do a very special thing unique to him. What a tragedy if that moment finds him unprepared for the work that would be his finest hour."

–Winston Churchill

Are you ready for your time? Are you getting prepared for your day of destiny? What are you doing now to get ready for the unique opportunities that are ahead? Realize that your hour of opportunity is coming. You will not get advance notice of its arrival. It will come to pass whether or not you are prepared for it. It will show itself suddenly. You cannot stall and scramble when the moment arrives. You will either be ready or riddled with regrets. With just a little forethought and planning, you can devote a small amount of time each day to concretely move forward in the direction of your dream, getting prepared for your hour of opportunity. In just one year, you can dramatically change your expertise. Set goals and define a concrete action plan to move forward. Are you reading on a consistent basis, expanding your knowledge? Are you scheduling time to devote to practice, to sharpen and hone your skills? Are you taking additional courses? Are you learning another language? Are you working with a mentor? Are you improving your communication skills? Do not squander the time at hand. This is your season for preparation. Don't let time-wasters consume the hours that should be devoted to your preparation. Time can either work for you or against you. Get ready for your opportunity. Get ready for your day. Your time is coming!

Be on guard! Be alert! You do not know when that time will come... If he comes suddenly, do not let him find you sleeping.

Mark 13:33, 36 (NIV)

DAY 10 | P.M.

DO YOUR HOMEWORK

"If you don't do your homework,
you won't make your free throws."

*–Larry Bird, Hall of Fame
NBA Basketball Legend*

What separates the good, from the great, and the great from the legendary? Often it comes down to the smallest of measures – a millisecond difference on the clock, or one point on the scoreboard. But that legendary difference was secured through tremendous sacrifices of time and painstaking effort committed to continually perfecting the most mundane of fundamentals. You may be in obscurity today. Do your homework. Perfect your fundamentals. And at the moment of destiny, your greatness, your legend will be secure.

Power Principle

So Pharaoh sent for Joseph, and he was quickly brought from the dungeon... Pharaoh said to Joseph, "I had a dream, and no one can interpret it. But I have heard it said of you that when you hear a dream you can interpret it." "I cannot do it," Joseph replied to Pharaoh, "but God will give Pharaoh the answer he desires..." "... God has revealed to Pharaoh what he is about to do... "And now let Pharaoh look for a discerning and wise man and put him in charge of the land of Egypt..." So Pharaoh asked them, "Can we find anyone like this man, one in whom is the spirit of God?" Then Pharaoh said to Joseph, "Since God has made all this known to you, there is no one so discerning and wise as you. You shall be in charge of my palace, and all my people are to submit to your orders. Only with respect to the throne will I be greater than you."

Genesis 41:14-16, 25, 33, 38-40 (NIV)

Power Thoughts

____

____

Action Step

____

____

DAY 11 | A.M.

PUT IT IN "D" FOR DAILY DISCIPLINE

"Decisions are made in a moment,
but growth comes by daily discipline."
–John Maxwell

Decisions are like turning the key in the ignition to start your engine. Decisions bring the fire to your dreams and goals, igniting your intentions and declaring your destiny. Once the decision is made, growth and progress are measured in the more mundane miles of your daily journey. You will only reach your destiny if you put in the miles! Are you sitting there just idling, listening to the purr of the engine, talking up your dreams? Or are you making real progress, mile by mile? Stop just sitting there! Shift gears, and put it in "D" for Daily Discipline! Discipline yourself to move forward daily, and you will arrive at your destination of success!

The sluggard craves and gets nothing, but the desires of the diligent are fully satisfied.

Proverbs 13:4 (NIV)

DAY 11 | P.M.

TAME THE TIME-WASTERS

"Time is neutral, but it can be made the ally of those who will seize it and use it to the full."
–Winston Churchill

Are you making the most of your time? Your time is the most precious resource you are given. If you lose money on an investment or business deal, you can make it back. However, if you waste your time, it is gone forever. You can never get back the time that you waste or squander. It is lost! Are you making time your ally or your enemy? To be successful, you must own the fact that you are solely responsible for managing your time. Guard and manage this most precious gateway to your goals. Mastering time management is one of the most essential skills you must develop. Plan your time. Schedule your highest priorities first. Make personal appointments on your calendar to seek direction, strategize, and solidify your ideas. Make appointments for your fitness time, family time, and friendship time. Schedule time to work on all of your projects and goals, and do not deviate from these appointments. Time bandits, like a swarm of locusts, will always come to eat up your treasured resource, but you must guard the time that you have committed to your highest priorities. Are you giving away your time to the time-wasters? Are you aimlessly watching hours of television? Is your time siphoned off through your online social networking? Is your time ticking away while you talk on the phone? What are your time wasters? Too much shopping or just hanging out with the fellas? To take new territory, take back your time. Tame the time-wasters!

Escape quickly from the company of fools; they're a waste of your time, a waste of your words.

Proverbs 14:7 (The Message)

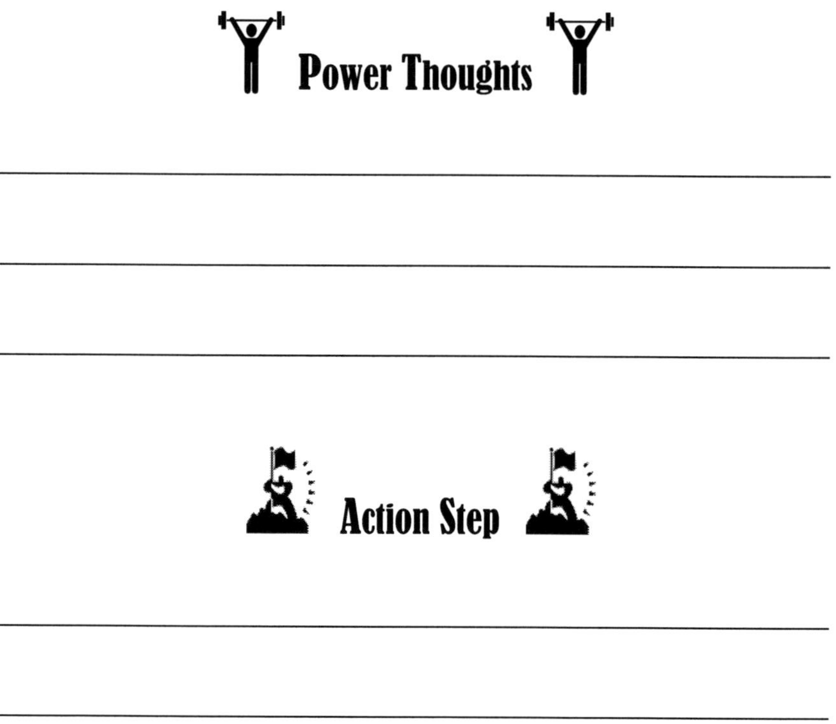

DAY 12 | A.M.

EXPECT THE BEST

"The greatest discovery of any generation is that a human being can alter his life by altering his attitude."
–William James

What are you expecting today? Set your mind to expect the best! You command the tone for your day, your year, and your life. Do not wait for events to unfold. Make the decision in advance to expect the best. Make the commitment to pull every ounce of positivity out of the day before it ever begins. Declare what your day will have in store. It is not the circumstances that arise that matter, it is how you choose to interpret them and respond to them that will dictate the direction of your day and your life. Are you expecting to struggle or to soar? Are you expecting trouble or triumph? Ask yourself, *"What is the best that can happen today?"* Expect good breaks. Expect to make a great business connection. Expect to have something positive happen unexpectedly. Expect to finish your project on time. Expect to close the deal. Expect that your proposal will be welcomed. Expect to have more energy and to feel better. Expect to enjoy the visit with your in-laws. Expect your children to do well in school, and to listen to your counsel. Expect creative ideas to flow into your mind. Expect to find the answer to a difficult problem. Do you have an attitude of expectancy? Wake up each day ready to win. Command the day to line up with your expectations. Command your mind to find the good in every situation. Take control of your thoughts throughout the day, and make them align with your expectations. You can change your life by changing your attitude. Expect the best!

Power Principle

God can do anything, you know—far more than you could ever imagine or guess or request in your wildest dreams! He does it not by pushing us around but by working within us, his Spirit deeply and gently within us.

Ephesians 3:20 (The Message)

Power Thoughts

____

____

Action Step

____

____

DAY 12 | P.M.

DEVELOP AN ATTITUDE OF EXCELLENCE

"If you are going to achieve excellence in big things, you develop the habit in little matters. Excellence is not an exception, it is a prevailing attitude."
–Colin Powell, The first African American Secretary of State in U.S. History

Do you have an attitude of excellence? How do you approach the little things? Having the attitude that "this is good enough" will rob you of essential practice in developing the attitude of excellence. You are developing a habit. Are you developing a habit of excellence or mediocrity? You cannot turn on excellence like a light switch. If you develop habits of laziness, slothfulness, and compromise, you will not be able to turn those off at will. If you have a lax attitude now in the small things, you will be sloppy and slipshod when the bigger opportunities come. Ultimately, you will be disqualified from the greatest opportunities that require excellence as a prerequisite. As an employee, are you slacking off at work, yet promising yourself you will work hard when you have your own company? I guarantee that you will seriously struggle in your own endeavor if you are not developing the success habits of discipline, diligence, and excellence now. Choose to be excellent in the little things. Look at how you care for your home, your car, and your clothes. Do you present yourself with excellence? Evaluate how you approach your projects at work. How do you approach your volunteer service? Every day, you are given multiple opportunities to rise to excellence. Break free from being just good enough. You can rise higher. Develop an attitude of excellence!

Then Daniel was brought in before the king. The king spoke, and said to Daniel, "Are you that Daniel who is one of the captives from Judah, whom my father the king brought from Judah? I have heard of you, that the Spirit of God is in you, and that light and understanding and excellent wisdom are found in you."

Daniel 5:13-14 (NKJV)

DAY 13 | A.M.

WHAT ARE YOU WAITING FOR?

"Life is not a spectator sport. If you're going to spend your whole life in the grandstand just watching what goes on, in my opinion you're wasting your life."

–Jackie Robinson, The first African American Major League Baseball player of the modern era

What are you waiting for? *"My schedule is so hectic…when things settle down I will get started." "I'm waiting for the economy to turn around." "I'm waiting to see what's going to happen with my job." "When the kids are back in school…" "I am waiting for him to apologize." "I'm going to start working out next week." "When I get married…"* One of the biggest traps that you will need to avoid on your way to an exceptional life is the myth of the more opportune time. When you put off pursuing what you truly want in life, whether it is a different career, financial independence, a more loving relationship, or a healthier body, you are allowing the myth of the more opportune time to defeat you. The fallacy of the more opportune time can cause you to delay your goals for weeks, months, and years. It's a favorite tool of your nemesis…Procrastination. The myth of the more opportune time will lull you into a holding pattern of waiting… and waiting…and waiting. There you are, sitting and waiting for circumstances to align in your favor. The problem is, that won't ever happen. There will never be a more convenient time or a less hectic time. The only time you have is NOW. Decide today to start taking action to move toward your goals. Stop waiting. There will never be a better time than right now. What are you waiting for?

What are you waiting for? Return to your God! Commit yourself in love, in justice! Wait for your God, and don't give up on him—ever!

Hosea 12:6 (The Message)

DAY 13 | P.M.

PUSH PAST PROCRASTINATION

"When you have a great and difficult task, something perhaps almost impossible, if you only work a little at a time, every day a little, suddenly the work will finish itself."

–Isak Dinesen

Are you procrastinating? When faced with a difficult or complex task, human nature is to put it off. To beat procrastination, first ask yourself, *"Why am I avoiding this?"* If you are avoiding it because you are anxious about the size or complexity of the task ahead, break it down into small, individual action items. Then, most importantly, choose one action you can accomplish right now. Commit to write one paragraph, to make one phone call, or to contact one potential client. Then do it! You will move from someday to now, you will release the momentum of starting, and you will feel the rush of achievement! Commit to do one action each day, and continue moving forward one step at a time. Before you know it, the task will be done! Fulfill the next action to finish! You can push past procrastination.

Power Principle

Hezekiah organized the groups of priests and Levites for their respective tasks, handing out job descriptions for conducting the services of worship: making the various offerings, and making sure that thanks and praise took place wherever and whenever GOD was worshiped. He also designated his personal contribution for the Whole-Burnt-Offerings for the morning and evening worship, for Sabbaths, for New Moon festivals, and for the special worship days set down in The Revelation of GOD.

2 Chronicles 31:2-3 (The Message)

Power Thoughts

Action Step

DAY 14 | A.M.

LET IT GO!

"It takes a lot of courage to release the familiar and seemingly secure, to embrace the new. But there is no real security in what is no longer meaningful. There is more security in the adventurous and exciting, for in movement there is life, and in change there is power."

–Alan Cohen

What are you holding onto that is holding you back? Are you hunkered down in a dead-end job you do not like because you have passively accepted the limiting belief that in the present economy, you can't make a change or rise any higher? Are you staying in a toxic, dangerous, or dry relationship because it's familiar, and you are afraid to be alone? Are you procrastinating on getting started on your goals and plans because deep down you are fearful of failure, rejection, or success? Summon your courage and inner strength, and choose to let it go. Let go of the past. Let go of false security. Let go of what is less than you desire and deserve. Embrace your passion and purpose. Embrace new opportunities. Choose to live, not languish. Step forward into action, adventure, and a new altitude. Take charge of your own future. Take back your power to change. Allow faith to guide you through uncertainty. You are most secure when you are using the fullness of your gifts and abilities to move in the direction of your dream and vision for your life. It's time. Let it go, and make the change!

Power Principle

So don't you see that we don't owe this old do-it-yourself life one red cent. There's nothing in it for us, nothing at all. The best thing to do is give it a decent burial and get on with your new life. God's Spirit beckons. There are things to do and places to go!

Romans 8:12-14 (The Message)

Power Thoughts

Action Step

DAY 14 | P.M.

CHANGE THE CHANNEL

"When one door of happiness closes, another opens; but often we look so long at the closed door that we do not see the one which has been opened for us."

–Helen Keller

Are you stuck? Are you frozen in time, looking at an opportunity past, wishing it had turned out differently? Are you stuck replaying the job lay-off, the end of the relationship, or the business deal that fell through? How many times are you going to watch that program? It doesn't end any differently no matter how many times you watch it. How many more times are you going to tell your friends and family the dramatic story line? How long will you sit there rewinding and replaying, again and again? Turn it off! Turn off the re-runs of your past, and change the channel! Free yourself of the failure fixation. Otherwise, you run the risk of missing completely the new opportunities that have already been set before you. Tune in to the premiere of your next life adventure! Tune in to the possibilities and new pathways. Fix your mind to see the business you can now build. Embrace the new career you can now wholeheartedly prepare for. See the healthy friendships you can now cultivate. See the bigger picture that encompasses a brighter future. To succeed, you must shake off defeat, discouragement, and disappointment. Trust that your trial will ultimately lead to triumph. Look with expectancy for the open door and confidently walk through it. To change your life, change the channel!

Power Principle

Forget about what's happened; don't keep going over old history. Be alert, be present. I'm about to do something brand-new. It's bursting out! Don't you see it? There it is! I'm making a road through the desert, rivers in the badlands.

Isaiah 43:18-19 (The Message)

Power Thoughts

Action Step

DAY 15 | A.M.

TAKE A TIME OUT, THEN TAKE NEW TERRITORY

"Learn to relax. Your body is precious, as it houses your mind and spirit. Inner peace begins with a relaxed body."

–Norman Vincent Peale

Listening to your body and heeding its call for rest and restoration are essential skills for sustaining success over the long haul. Over 75% of all illnesses are stress related. Long term exposure to chronic stress can lead to serious health problems including high blood pressure, a suppressed immune system, increased risk of heart attack and stroke, digestive problems, sleep problems, obesity, and depression. To face daily frustrations and deadlines, or tough challenges like a job change, financial pressure, or increased work responsibilities, be sensitive to your body's signals for restoration, and honor its natural cycles. Set aside one day a week to give your body complete rest from work and commitments, enjoying family and friends instead. Get a full night's sleep to avoid sleep deprivation. Schedule short relaxation breaks each day: take a walk, enjoy a bubble bath, read a book, or listen to music. Breathe deeply and be quiet for five minutes to interrupt a stressful situation. Take a time out, then take new territory!

Power Principle

Remember to observe the Sabbath day by keeping it holy. You have six days each week for your ordinary work, but the seventh day is a Sabbath day of rest dedicated to the LORD your God. On that day no one in your household may do any work...For in six days the LORD made the heavens, the earth, the sea, and everything in them; but on the seventh day he rested. That is why the LORD blessed the Sabbath day and set it apart as holy.

Exodus 20:8-11 (NLT)

Power Thoughts

____

____

____

Action Step

____

____

Day 15 | P.M.

REST TO RISE HIGHER

"I still need more healthy rest in order to work at my best. My health is the main capital I have and I want to administer it intelligently."

–Ernest Hemingway

Are you pressing forward to accomplish your goals, to ignite your creativity, or solve a tough challenge? REST! Each day, allow your body to rejuvenate, refresh, and recover. Sleep deprivation can contribute to weight gain, diabetes, high blood pressure, and heart attacks. The body restores itself during sleep. Neurotoxins are neutralized, cells divide, tissue synthesizes, and growth hormones are released. During Rapid Eye Movement (REM) sleep, important information is locked into more permanent memory. Studies show that when people are deprived of REM sleep, they are less adept at creative problem solving. To do your best work, schedule time to rest and take care of your body. Eat healthy, nutritious foods, exercise 4-6 times per week, and ensure you get a full night's sleep of 7-8 hours, consistently. Rest and recover to reach your pinnacle. Rest to rise higher!

Power Principle

Unless the LORD builds a house, the work of the builders is wasted. Unless the LORD protects a city, guarding it with sentries will do no good. It is useless for you to work so hard from early morning until late at night, anxiously working for food to eat; for God gives rest to his loved ones.

Psalm 127:1-2 (NLT)

Power Thoughts

Action Step

DAY 16 | A.M.

TELL YOURSELF TO TRIUMPH!

"Talk back to your internal critic."
–Robert McCain

Is your self-talk sabotaging your success? Are you confident or critical? Are you focused on your fumbles, and fixated on your failures? Do you meditate on your mistakes and rehearse your regrets? Do you easily list your limitations, yet struggle to see your strengths? Self-doubting self-talk cannot be allowed to run rampant in your mind. To rise to victory, you must command your thought life to announce your achievement in advance of its fulfillment. To bring forth your destiny, you must see it, say it, and believe it. You must see yourself as well able to achieve your goals. Declare your determination to succeed. What you focus on will increase. What you meditate on gains momentum. What you mentally envision will manifest. Stop listening to your internal critic. Your past is over. Silence your accuser. When you hear the criticism rising within you, talk back! Talk back to the doubter, who delights in your downturns. Talk back to your internal critic, who celebrates your setbacks. Silence the cynic, who replays your worst days. Let courage counsel you when you are fearful or uncertain. Let confidence speak boldly on your soundtrack of self-talk. Mold your mindset. Speak your success. Tell yourself who you are. Tell yourself you are about to take new territory. Tell yourself you are well able to accomplish your goals. Tell yourself you are determined to finish. Tell yourself to triumph!

Power Principle

Death and life are in the power of the tongue, And those who love it will eat its fruit.

Proverbs 18:21 (NKJV)

Power Thoughts

Action Step

DAY 16 | P.M.

THIS IS IT

"The truth is that our finest moments are most likely to occur when we are feeling deeply uncomfortable, unhappy, or unfulfilled. For it is only in such moments, propelled by our discomfort, that we are likely to step out of our ruts and start searching for different ways or truer answers."

–M. Scott Peck

There is a day that will come when you will decide enough is enough. In your hour of anguish and frustration, you will make a decision that you deserve better. There is a moment that will speak to you louder than any other moment of your life. *"This is not acceptable."* In that moment you will declare, *"This is it. I have had enough. I can do more than this. I deserve better than this. I can rise higher than where I am now."* In this moment you will stop coping. In this moment, you will stop minimizing. *"It's not so bad."* In this moment you will see it for what it really is, and you will be ready to take a stand. This is the precise moment that everything will change for you. This is the moment when you prepare for battle. You will look up and finally see your future. You will see your summit. You will dig deep and summon your courage and confidence. You will call upon your drive and determination. You will ignite your passion. You will fuel your will to fight. You will take a stand. You will step out. You will search for the solution. You will make a bold move. You will conquer your fears. You will break off your bonds, and shatter your shackles. Welcome to your liberation. You are now free. This is it!

Just then a woman who had suffered for twelve years with constant bleeding came up behind him. She touched the fringe of his robe, for she thought, "If I can just touch his robe, I will be healed." Jesus turned around, and when he saw her he said, "Daughter, be encouraged! Your faith has made you well." And the woman was healed at that moment.

Matthew 9:20-22 (NLT)

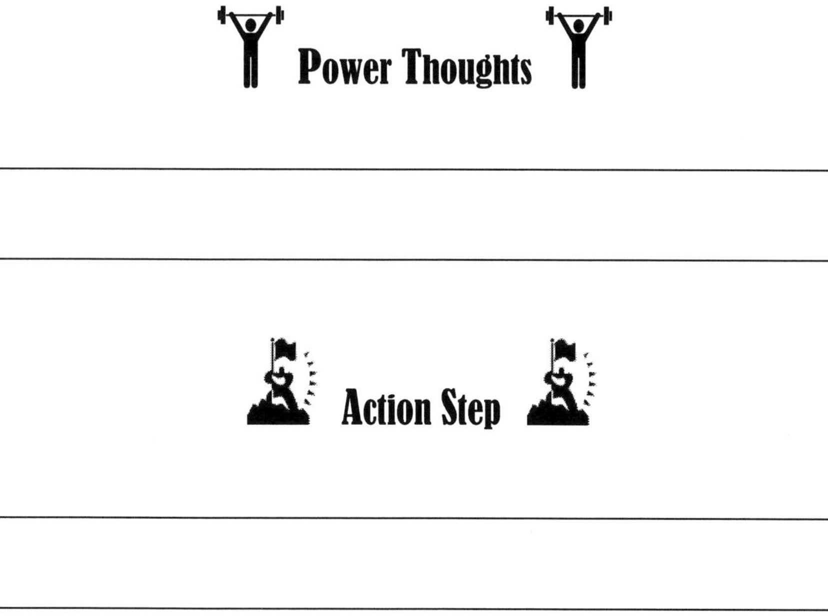

DAY 17 | A.M.

WHAT IS IN YOUR HAND?

"Do what you can,
with what you have, where you are."
–Theodore Roosevelt

Learning to see the richness of the resources you already possess is a master key to your success. What can you do now, today, with what you already have to move forward toward your dreams and goals? Don't get trapped in the quicksand of comparison, lamenting the talents, gifts, and opportunities of others while overlooking your very own. You are not lacking! You are abounding with unique opportunities and untapped talents. Take an inventory of your strengths, gifts, and resources. Open your eyes to your own opportunities. Which abilities come naturally and effortlessly that you can use today? Who is in your network? Which life experiences can you build on? Which talents can you begin to refine and develop? Do not delay the pursuit of your dreams and goals because you believe you are unqualified to do so. The craving for more credentials will cause you to discredit what you already know and what you already can do. This can become a pursuit of validation rather than education. You are already well equipped and qualified to begin! Make a list of actions you can do now, and begin today. Yes, you should always seek to gain more knowledge, skills, and strategies, but completing that objective is not a precursor to reporting to your starting line. Set your goals and GO! Learning is a lifelong journey. Take the additional courses, add the new skills, and complete the certifications concurrently as you pursue your goals. Do what you can, with what you have, where you are. What is in your hand?

"Moses objected, "They won't trust me. They won't listen to a word I say...." So God said, "What's that in your hand?" "A staff," Moses replied. ... "And who do you think made the human mouth? ... Isn't it I, God? So, get going. I'll be right there with you…I'll be right there to teach you what to say."

Exodus 4:1, 2, 11, 12 (The Message)

DAY 17 | P.M.

DON'T YOU DARE COMPARE!

"A thoroughbred horse never looks at the other horses. It just concentrates on running the fastest race it can."

–Henry Fonda

Are you crippled by comparison? Don't you dare compare yourself to others! When you fall into the comparison trap, you devalue all of the differences that make you unique. You become blind to your own brilliance! Celebrate your own uniqueness. Be comfortable in your own skin. There has never been, and there will never be, another person like you. Diane Roger put it this way: "You are an unrepeatable miracle." Concentrate on the gifting that is inside of you. Let your gifts shine brightly! You have everything you need to succeed. Why would you want to copy anyone else? Be the original you! Don't look to the successes or failures of others to measure your personal progress. Measure yourself against your own potential. Always strive for your personal best. Did someone finish college before you, get promoted ahead of you, or get married before you? Don't you dare compare! Run your own race. Enjoy your seasons and accomplishments as they come. There is a reason things happen in the seasons and times that they do. Embrace your own pace. Run the best race you can possibly run. Press forward to fulfill your personal potential. Don't you dare compare!

Pay careful attention to your own work, for then you will get the satisfaction of a job well done, and you won't need to compare yourself to anyone else. For we are each responsible for our own conduct.

Galatians 6:4-5 (NLT)

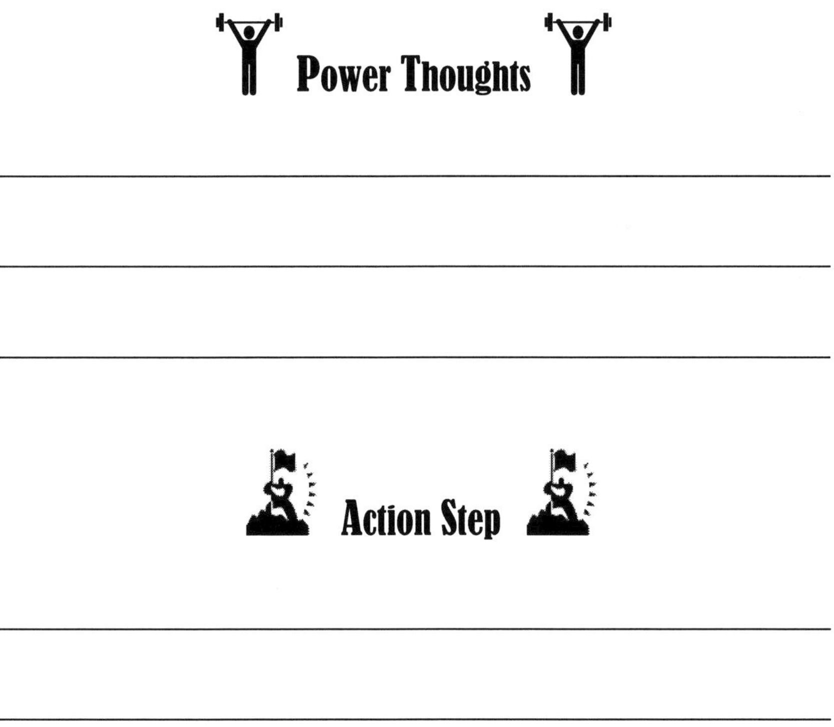

DAY 18 | A.M.

IMPLEMENT YOUR IDEAS

"Ideas won't keep:
something must be done about them."
–Alfred North Whitehead

Interrupting your routine thoughts are priceless ideas that are the keys to solving your problems, fulfilling your goals, and unlocking your future. Are you listening? Many great ideas are missed or dismissed in the static of the status quo daily routine. Do you have an idea for a new business, product, or service? An idea to streamline your household budget? An idea to solve a tough challenge on your job? Or, an idea to differentiate yourself with a potential new employer? Some ideas are brash and persistent, while others are subtle and fleeting, but all are perishable. They will die without action. What are you doing to bring your ideas to life? Cultivate your creativity. Develop the habit of writing down your ideas. Select an action you can take today to move ahead. The battle is won when something is done! Implement your ideas!

"For My thoughts are not your thoughts, Nor are your ways My ways," says the LORD. "For as the heavens are higher than the earth, So are My ways higher than your ways, And My thoughts than your thoughts.

Isaiah 55:8-9 (NKJV)

DAY 18 | P.M.

PRACTICE POSSIBILITY THINKING

"When you have exhausted all possibilities, remember this — you haven't."

–Thomas A. Edison

Challenges are gifts that place demands on your creativity, ingenuity, and tenacity to find new solutions. The key is to continue to ask yourself, *"What other options do I have? What other possibilities exist that I have not considered yet?"* Remove the limiting belief that there is only one way or a few ways to accomplish your goals. If you succumb to believing you do not have any other course of action, your mind will stop looking for a new possibility! You were created with an unlimited capacity to invent. Practice possibility thinking!

Power Principle

"Jesus looked at them and said, "With man this is impossible, but not with God; all things are possible with God."

Mark 10:27 (NIV)

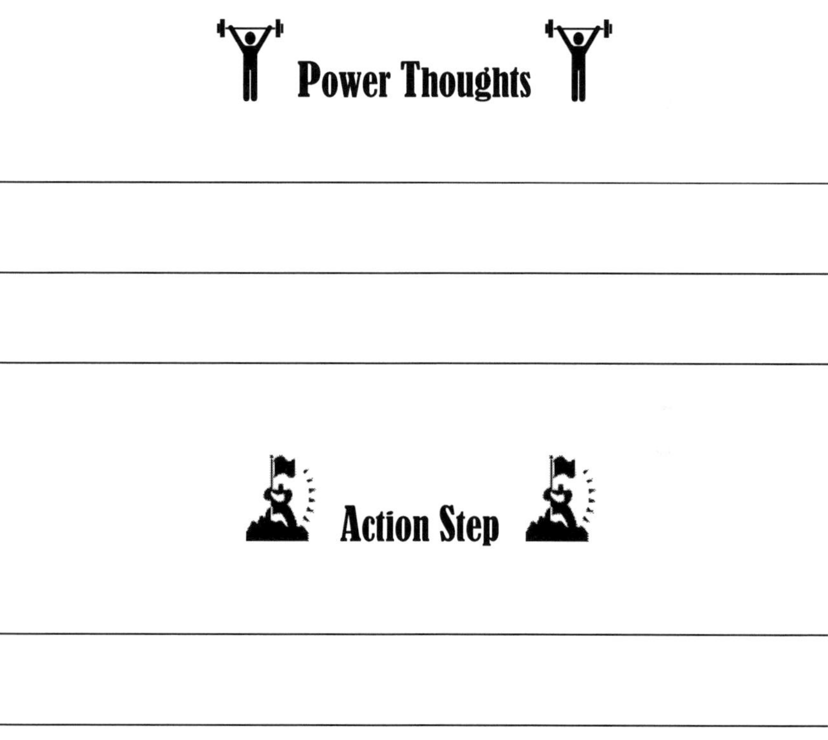

Power Thoughts

Action Step

DAY 19 | A.M.

TAKE YOUR SHOT

"You miss 100% of the shots you never take."
–Wayne Gretzky

Success will be presented to you in a series of isolated opportunities that manifest suddenly, show themselves briefly, and often close quickly. Being hesitant and indecisive will cost you. There is no room for you to be timid and tentative. A victor doesn't vacillate; a warrior will not waver. It's time to step up. It's time to take your chance. Take your shot! When taken confidently and courageously, these opportunities will combine and compound, giving momentum to your mission, and substance to your success. *"What if I miss? What if I fail? What if I fall?"* What if it works? What if you score? What if you succeed? What if you win! If you miss, learn from it, adjust your strategy, and prepare for the next opportunity. You won't make them all, but to do nothing will guarantee your defeat. See and seize your opportunity! Take your shot. You will never know the success that is well within your reach if you continue to falter and fret. Opportunities are fleeting. You cannot win when you hedge and hesitate. Prepare to prosper. Set your mind to succeed! Visualize your victory. Take aim at your goal. You will not be denied. Take your shot!

Power Principle

Then Caleb quieted the people before Moses, and said, "Let us go up at once and take possession, for we are well able to overcome it."

Numbers 13:30 (NKJV)

Power Thoughts

Action Step

DAY 19 | P.M.

JUST SHOW UP!

"Eighty percent of success is just showing up."
–Woody Allen

You may not have it all figured out yet. That's OK! Most people will not dare step out and try. Paralyzed by procrastination, over-planning, or perpetual preparation, they never arrive at the starting line. To achieve the extraordinary, you must get in the game in the first place! Show up and give your best effort. Just show up. You will be among a select few that will even attempt a new future. What you do not know now you will learn through the experience! You will learn quickly and make the adjustments. Use the best plan you have available now. Pack it up and proceed. Get going. You can't win if you don't begin. Just show up!

A man's mind plans his way, but the Lord directs his steps and makes them sure.

Proverbs 16:9 (AMP)

DAY 20 | A.M.

RAISE YOUR EXPECTATIONS

"The greater danger for most of us lies not in setting our aim too high and falling short; but in setting our aim too low, and achieving our mark."

–Michelangelo di Lodovico Buonarroti Simoni

Michelangelo, the extraordinary sculptor, painter, architect, and poet of the Italian Renaissance created many of the most renowned and influential artistic works in history, including the Statue of David, the Statue of Moses, and the ceiling of the Sistine Chapel, which took approximately four years to complete. He sculpted his most famous work, the Statue of David, when he was 29 years old, yet at 74 he succeeded Antonio da Sangallo the Younger as the architect of Saint Peter's Basilica. What is the vision for your life? What are you striving to achieve? Challenge yourself to raise your expectations! Stir up your unique gifts and abilities. Stretch yourself to see a bigger plan for your life. Expand your boundaries. There are greater accomplishments that are destined to emerge from your passionate pursuit of your purpose. What is stopping you from reaching higher? Comparison will cause you to limit your personal expectations by measuring your future against the achievements of your colleagues, friends, and peers. Comfort will caress you with complacent thinking. *"Take it easy, be satisfied, you've done well, let's maintain things just the way they are."* Critical commentary from people who do not understand your mission will make you play small, to not stand out from the crowd or draw attention to your boldness. Complications will challenge your will to win; setbacks will test your tenacity. When faced with these challenges, remember Michelangelo. Pursue your personal best. Raise your expectations!

Power Principle

"Before I shaped you in the womb, I knew all about you. Before you saw the light of day, I had holy plans for you…"

Jeremiah 1:5 (The Message)

DAY 20 | P.M.

SKIP THE SHORTCUTS

"There are no shortcuts
to any place worth going."
–Beverly Sills

The obsessive search for the shortcut, the lucky break, and the get-rich-quick scheme costs more money, time, and energy than committing to a proven system of success, while producing no results and worst of all, no character! Decide today to stop searching for ease and comfort. Even if the shortcut worked (and it won't) you would not value the end result. The greatest fulfillment in life comes from overcoming the obstacles, being courageous in the face of challenges, rising above adversity, and succeeding over setbacks. The shortcut makes you weak, and ultimately costs you the person you could have become if you would have stood tall and taken on the challenge. Skip the shortcuts!

Power Principle

Good planning and hard work lead to prosperity, but hasty shortcuts lead to poverty.

Proverbs 21:5 (NLT)

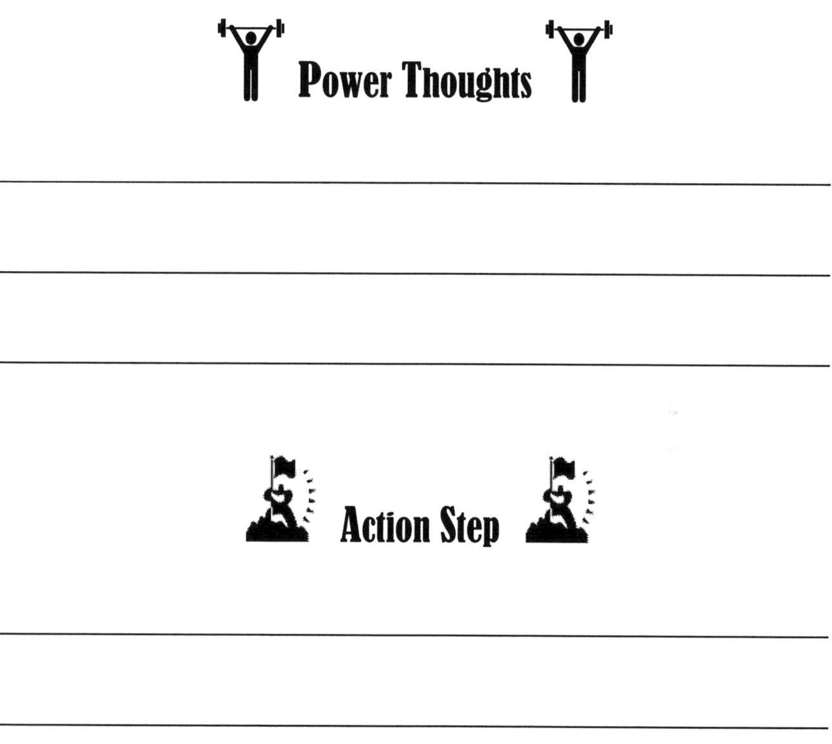

Power Thoughts

Action Step

DAY 21 | A.M.

YOU ARE GETTING STRONGER

"One who gains strength by overcoming obstacles possesses the only strength which can overcome adversity."

–Albert Schweitzer

What is your attitude toward problems and difficulties? Are you irritated and agitated with every challenge that comes? How do you respond to the day-to-day challenges that you face? Do you wish they would just go away? Do you long for a life with no issues? Consider this: a life with no challenges would be ideal if you want to be weak. When a major hardship arises, you will be ill-prepared and powerless, having no option but to roll over, showing your soft underbelly of surrender. Without consistent practice at solving problems, you cannot prepare for the day of adversity, and stand confidently, knowing you are well able to rise to any challenge. To develop strength and power, change your attitude toward problems! The problem comes to prepare you for greater victories ahead. With each small challenge you overcome, you are getting stronger. With each crisis conquered, you are getting stronger. When you face an obstacle, say to yourself, *"I willingly take this on. I will resolve this problem. I am getting stronger!"* You are preparing for bigger battles. You are in training for tougher times. When the day of adversity comes, you will stand confidently, knowing you are fully prepared for this moment, and with strength and courage, you will face your greatest foe and you will emerge victorious. Don't cower from a challenge. Face it head on. You are getting stronger!

Power Principle

David said to Saul, "Let no one lose heart on account of this Philistine; your servant will go and fight him." Saul replied, "You are not able to go out against this Philistine and fight him; you are only a boy..." But David said to Saul, "Your servant has been keeping his father's sheep. When a lion or a bear came and carried off a sheep from the flock, I went after it... Your servant has killed both the lion and the bear; this uncircumcised Philistine will be like one of them, because he has defied the armies of the living God. The LORD who delivered me from the paw of the lion and the paw of the bear will deliver me from the hand of this Philistine."

1 Samuel 17:32-37 (NIV) David, as he prepared to defeat Goliath

Power Thoughts

____

____

Action Step

____

____

DAY 21 | P.M.

STICK WITH IT

"My God-given talent is my ability to stick with something longer than anyone else."
–Herschel Walker, Heisman Trophy Winner

Will you stay the course to fulfill your dreams? Will you persevere through challenges, setbacks, and discouragement? Will you maintain your commitment to your success habits even when you are not seeing the tangible results just yet? Stick with it! You will reap the benefit and see the reward if you do not lose hope! When challenges arise, reassess your strategy, adjust your plan, but do not abort your mission. Do not quit. Never give up. Stay the course. Hold fast to your vision, and it will come to pass. Stick with it!

So don't throw it all away now. You were sure of yourselves then. It's still a sure thing! But you need to stick it out, staying with God's plan so you'll be there for the promised completion. It won't be long now, he's on the way; he'll show up most any minute. But anyone who is right with me thrives on loyal trust; if he cuts and runs, I won't be very happy. But we're not quitters who lose out. Oh, no! We'll stay with it and survive, trusting all the way.

Hebrews 10:35-39 (The Message)

Power Thoughts

____

____

____

Action Step

____

____

DAY 22 | A.M.

PRIORITIZE TO PROSPER

"Don't tell me where your priorities are. Show me where you spend your money and I'll tell you what they are."
–James W. Frick

What are your money priorities? Are you an investor or consumer? Which one is your priority? Are you investing in yourself and your future? If you aren't happy with where you are financially, look at what you are consuming vs. what you are investing. The problem is not a lack of money, but doing the wrong things with the money that you already have. To climb higher, you will have to make some changes in how you think and how you invest. View the money used to create a pathway to prosperity as an investment and not as an expense. Successful people recognize investment opportunities that present themselves in the form of books, courses, coaches, and seminars. Are you quick to say you can't afford an investment into your future, but you will move heaven and earth to buy the latest consumer electronics or brand name handbag? Look down at your shoes. Have you spent more to dress up your feet than to press toward your future? Do a self-assessment.

Pull out your checkbook and your credit card statements for the last year. Did you spend more on lattes than you invested in learning? Have you spent more on your car than you've invested in your craft? Do you spend more on your nails than you invest in knowledge? Do you see why you are not moving forward financially? Make it a priority to invest in the opportunities that will transform your financial future. Curtail your consuming! Start investing in yourself. Prioritize to prosper!

Power Principle

But store up for yourselves treasures in heaven, where moth and rust do not destroy, and where thieves do not break in and steal. For where your treasure is, there your heart will be also.

Matthew 6:20-21 (NIV)

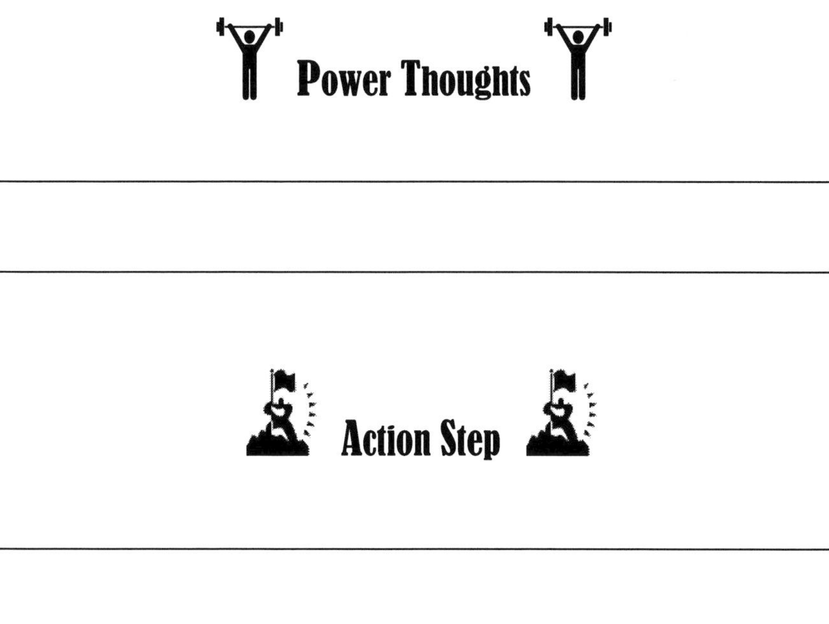

Power Thoughts

____

____

Action Step

____

____

DAY 22 | P.M.

PUT YOUR HEART INTO IT!

"We're not sent into this world to do anything into which we cannot put our hearts."
–John Ruskin

Are you giving your all? Are you putting everything you have into your work? Exceptional people are those who put extraordinary effort into ordinary tasks. Everything you do deserves your best effort and an attitude of excellence. Check your attitude. Everything you produce has your name on it! Do you have a signature of success? Does your signature read "Spectacular"? Is your autograph "Amazing"? Give your all! Dial up your discipline, diligence, and drive. Press in with passion, purpose, and power. Put your heart into it! Leave a track record that testifies to your commitment to excellence. Don't shirk on the small things! Don't slack on the simple. Shine! Be outstanding. Use your best gifts, abilities, and skills. Bring your brilliance at every opportunity. Do the work you were designed to do, and give it all you have. Martin Luther King, Jr. said, "If a man is called to be a street sweeper, he should sweep streets even as Michelangelo painted, or Beethoven composed music, or Shakespeare wrote poetry. He should sweep streets so well that all the hosts of heaven and earth will pause to say, here lived a great street sweeper who did his job well." Choose to be extraordinary. Whatever is at your hand to do, give it your all. Put your heart into it!

Power Principle

Whatever you do, work at it with all your heart, as working for the Lord, not for men, since you know that you will receive an inheritance from the Lord as a reward. It is the Lord Christ you are serving.

Colossians 3:23-24 (NIV)

Power Thoughts

Action Step

DAY 23 | A.M.

SHAKE IT OFF!

"Whenever anyone has offended me, I try to raise my soul so high that the offense cannot reach it."

–Rene Descartes

Have you been offended? Has someone said something hateful or hurtful toward you? Shake it off! Offenses are like poisonous darts that can penetrate your heart and soul. To succeed, you must guard your heart from offenses. The offense will come, but you can choose not to internalize it. Do not let the words or actions seep into your soul. When your mind is clouded and your heart is polluted with an offense, you cannot do your best work. It's a distraction. Keep your self-concept shielded from attack. Shake off the opinions of others. Why does it matter? You know who you are. Shake off the unfair criticisms. Shake off the mocking comments. You are still going after your goals, regardless of what other people think. Shake off the rude comment or the insult. Let it go. Rise to a new level of confidence, so you are not vulnerable to offenses and injuries. Rise to a new level of compassion, so you are not seduced into holding a grudge. Forgive it and forget it. Offenses have a way of repeating themselves over and over again in your mind. One comment can distract you for hours or even days as you replay it, repeat it, and rehearse it. Don't get distracted or delayed from achieving your destiny by allowing an offense to hold you back. Stay focused. When the offense comes, shake it off!

Guard your heart above all else, for it determines the course of your life.

Proverbs 4:23 (NLT)

DAY 23 | P.M.

KEEP GOING AND GROWING

"No person is your friend who demands your silence, or denies your right to grow."

–Alice Walker

When you are compelled by your vision to move forward, the metamorphosis you are experiencing as you expand to fulfill your destiny will be readily seen by all of those around you. Some will accept the changes in you, and many will not. Do not be caught off guard by the actions of those who will resist your progress, attempting to arrest and hold you in your current state for their own comfort, security, or control. Have the courage to let them go and grow! A true friend discerns your new season, encourages your transformation, supports your vision, celebrates your victories, and gives you room to grow! To fulfill your destiny, keep going and GROWING!

Power Principle

Friends come and friends go, but a true friend sticks by you like family.

Proverbs 18:24 (The Message)

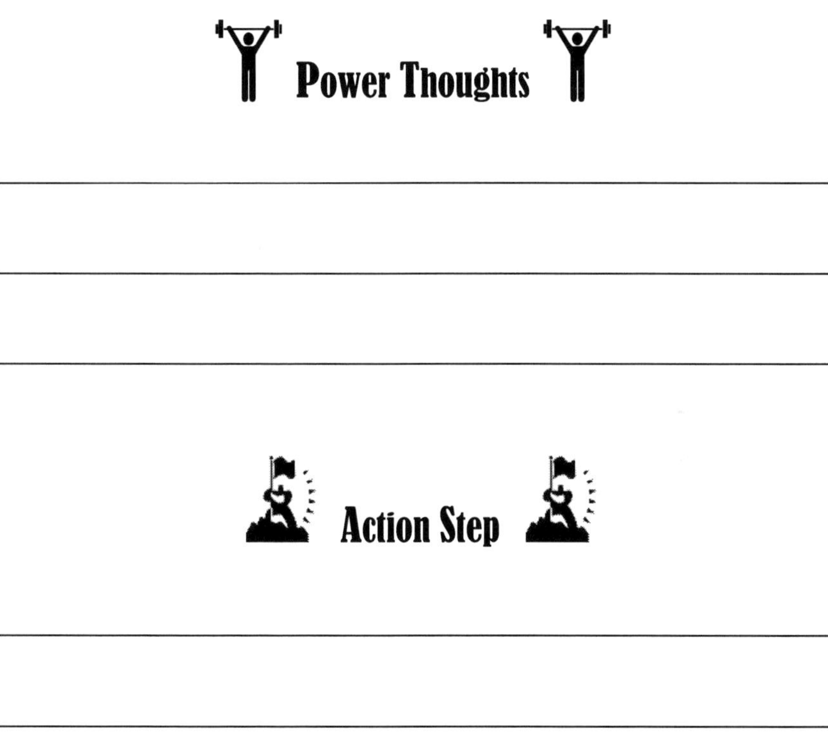

Power Thoughts

Action Step

DAY 24 | A.M.

EMBRACE YOUR PLAN B

"The most successful people are those who are good at plan B."

–James Yorke

The plan you start with is not the plan you are going to finish with! Make your plan to the best of your current knowledge and ability, then START! The power is in starting. Recognize that THE MOMENT you begin, you will have far more knowledge than you did when you were only planning. Then the power strategy of adjustment can kick into action. You will constantly feed the new knowledge gained through action into your plan. As you act, you will learn. As you learn, you will adjust. As you adjust, you will succeed! New opportunities, unforeseen circumstances, and changes beyond your control will cause you to constantly adjust. Be agile. Embrace your Plan B to succeed!

Power Principle

They went to Phrygia, and then on through the region of Galatia. Their plan was to turn west into Asia province, but the Holy Spirit blocked that route. So they went to Mysia and tried to go north to Bithynia, but the Spirit of Jesus wouldn't let them go there either. Proceeding on through Mysia, they went down to the seaport Troas. That night Paul had a dream: A Macedonian stood on the far shore and called across the sea, "Come over to Macedonia and help us!" The dream gave Paul his map. We went to work at once getting things ready to cross over to Macedonia. All the pieces had come together. We knew now for sure that God had called us to preach the good news to the Europeans.

Acts 16:6-10 (The Message)

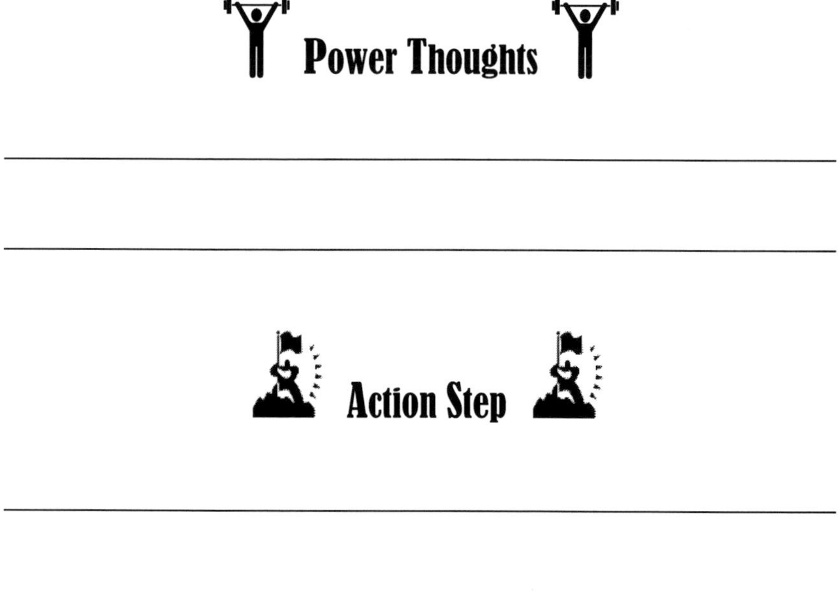

Power Thoughts

Action Step

DAY 24 | P.M.

SEIZE YOUR SUCCESS BY STARTING OVER

"Vitality shows not only in the ability to persist, but in the ability to start over."

–F. Scott Fitzgerald

When a failure, mistake, or setback happens, the sooner you learn from it, adjust your plan, and begin again, the faster you will decisively defeat the toxic *"I can't do it"* beliefs that will try to overtake your mind, stopping you from moving forward. Create a positive meaning to associate with the experience and embark again *immediately* toward your goal. What did you learn? How can you use that learning to your advantage? What will you do differently this time? Now shake it off, and start again! Seize your success by starting over!

Power Principle

God's gifts and God's call are under full warranty — never canceled, never rescinded.

Romans 11:29 (The Message)

Power Thoughts

Action Step

DAY 25 | A.M.

JUST SAY THANK YOU

"If the only prayer you said in your whole life was, 'thank you,' that would suffice."

–Meister Eckhart

What are you thankful for today? Constantly cultivating and living in an attitude of gratitude is a power strategy of success and ultimate fulfillment in life. Being thankful takes you out of scarcity, lack, fear, and anxiety, and puts you in a mindset of abundance, allowing you to recognize the thousands of blessings you have right now today. Thankfulness for all you have will change your perspective on your life, allowing you to enjoy the richness you already possess, and unlocking even greater blessings to flow into your life. When you consider your present wealth and blessings, you can relax and trust that the dreams and goals you are striving for will surely come to pass. Take time today to thank your Heavenly Father for your life, health, strength, safety, family, friends, home, food, talents, skills, abilities, and thousands of other blessings you have right now. You are already wealthy. Just say thank you!

Power Principle

Let all that I am praise the LORD; with my whole heart, I will praise his holy name. Let all that I am praise the LORD; may I never forget the good things he does for me. He forgives all my sins and heals all my diseases. He redeems me from death and crowns me with love and tender mercies. He fills my life with good things. My youth is renewed like the eagle's!

Psalm 103:1-5 (NLT)

Power Thoughts

Action Step

DAY 25 | P.M.

TAKE TIME TO APPRECIATE

"Appreciation can make a day, even change a life. Your willingness to put it into words is all that is necessary."

–Margaret Cousins

A successful person deeply contributes to the lives of others. Our most impactful contributions often occur in how we enrich the lives of the people we encounter on a daily basis. One of the deepest human needs is to be appreciated and valued. You can transform lives, starting today, by showing appreciation to the people that are so easy to take for granted. Challenge yourself to notice all who serve you, help you, encourage you, and bless you every day. Stop for 30 seconds and verbally express your appreciation and gratitude. Make "I appreciate you" one of the most commonly used phrases in your vocabulary. Write a handwritten letter of appreciation. Take five minutes and send a "Thank You" card today. Show heartfelt appreciation and watch lives change! You are never too busy to take time to acknowledge what others do on your behalf. Take time to appreciate!

Power Principle

Every time you cross my mind, I break out in exclamations of thanks to God. Each exclamation is a trigger to prayer. I find myself praying for you with a glad heart.

Philippians 1:3-4 (The Message)

Power Thoughts

Action Step

Day 26 | A.M.

KEEP GOING, YOUR BREAKTHROUGH IS CLOSE THAN YOU THINK

"Look at a stone cutter hammering away at his rock, perhaps a hundred times without as much as a crack showing in it. Yet at the hundred-and-first blow it will split in two, and I know it was not the last blow that did it, but all that had gone before."

–Jacob A. Riis

The journey to success cannot be seen with the naked eye. Most of it is traveled in obscurity, anonymity, repetition, tenacity, determination, and perseverance with no visible signs of change or progress. If you continue on the journey, you will succeed. Don't fall victim to evaluating your proximity to your breakthrough by what you can see. Trust the journey, trust the process, and keep going. Most people give up because of what they see or do not see. But you can only see part of the story. You cannot see all the changes that are happening in you beneath the surface. You cannot see what is happening beyond your line of sight, where circumstances are aligning in your favor. Despite what it looks like, do not give up.

You must use your eyes of faith and persevere. Just as the stone cutter trusts his process, you must trust your success habits. *"I've sent out 100 resumes but I still do not have a job offer."* Is your victory in the 101st resume? *"I've made 100 sales calls."* Will you close the 101st presentation? *"I've shown 100 houses."* Will you sell the 101st? With each attempt, you are getting stronger, you are sharpening your skills, you are finding the right contacts, you are eliminating the wrong options, you are closing in on the bulls-eye. Keep going! Your breakthrough is closer than you think!

Is not My word like fire [that consumes all that cannot endure the test]? says the Lord, and like a hammer that breaks in pieces the rock [of most stubborn resistance]?

Jeremiah 23:29 (AMP)

DAY 26 | P.M.

NEVER GIVE UP!

"Never give up. And never, under any circumstances, face the facts."
–Ruth Gordon

What do you do when it looks like all hope is lost? What do you do when everyone around you is telling you to face the facts - that it's time to give it up? You stand firm! You stand your ground. Never, ever give up. When your situation looks bleak, even hopeless, that is when you will have to dig down deep to an inner reservoir of strength called Resolve. When you have committed – truly committed - to your mission, and when you know you are doing exactly what you were brought into the earth to do, you have this steadfast strength on the inside of you. Resolve is the bedrock of your determination, endurance, perseverance, and tenacity. It is the inner commitment you have made that is immovable and immutable. It is the covenant you have made with yourself that you will not regress or retreat. When you are tested with failures, setbacks, and difficult circumstances, you must dig down and tap into your steel-willed determination to succeed. There will be days when you will have no other strength to rely on but your Resolve. What do you do when all logic is screaming at you to retreat? What do you say when the facts say you are failing? You stand firm. You stand your ground. When the situation appears impossible, it is your Resolve that says, *"With God, all things are possible. I will find an answer. I will endure the storm. I will keep the faith. I will keep standing. I will adjust my strategy. I will ask for help. I will listen to wise counsel. I will keep fighting. I will not give up. I will succeed."* Be steadfast and immovable. Dig deep into your reservoir of strength called Resolve. Never give up!

Power Principle

Therefore put on God's complete armor, that you may be able to resist and stand your ground on the evil day [of danger], and, having done all [the crisis demands], to stand [firmly in your place].

Ephesians 6:13 (AMP)

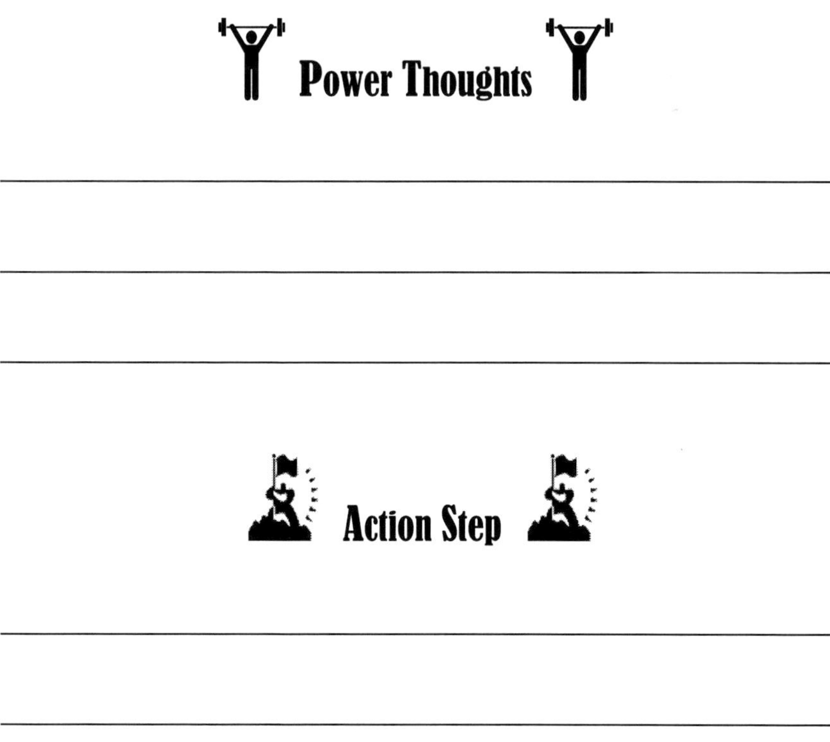

Power Thoughts

Action Step

Day 27 | A.M.

VALUES ARE VITAL

"The ultimate measure of a man is not where he stands in moments of comfort and convenience, but where he stands at times of challenge and controversy."
–Martin Luther King, Jr.

What are your core values? What are the deepest beliefs you hold that will guide you through times of testing, trial, and turbulence? Honesty and integrity? Justice and fairness? Courage and bravery? Loyalty and fidelity? Dependability and trustworthiness? Empathy and compassion? When you identify your core values, and determine what they mean to your life, you are setting up a rock solid decision-making system well in advance of any challenge or controversy. When you are faced with a shady business deal or foolish financial scheme, your core values of honesty and integrity will demolish the deal for you. When your co-worker gets flirtatious, inviting you out for drinks after work before you head home to your family, loyalty and faithfulness will implode the infidelity for you. When you witness discrimination and oppression, and it is within your power to stand up or keep silent, justice and fairness will cry out for you, moving you to action, no matter the cost. If you do not have a value system firmly established, situational ethics and shifting sentiments will drive your life into decay. Duality in your thinking will lead to your destruction. Many talented lives go down in fiery flames due to hidden indiscretions and habitual poor choices. A life laden with lapses in judgment is destined for failure. With all of the talents and skills you possess, your ability to stand strong on your firm foundation of guiding values may be the greatest gift of all. Your values are vital.

Power Principle

How much better to get wisdom than gold, to choose understanding rather than silver! The highway of the upright avoids evil; he who guards his way guards his life.

Proverbs 16:16-17 (NIV)

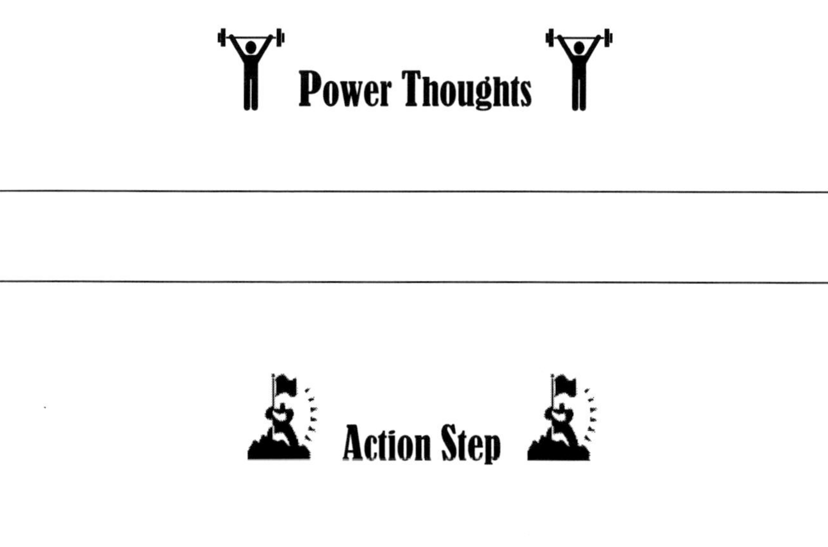

Power Thoughts

Action Step

DAY 27 | P.M.

IN ALL THINGS, YOU ARE A CHAMPION!

"Don't let other people tell you who you are."
–Diane Sawyer

In 1998, Michelle Kwan was the clear favorite to win Olympic gold. She skated valiantly, but her quest for Olympic gold was upset by Tara Lipinski when Tara became the first woman in Olympic history to perform a triple loop in combination with another triple loop. Asked repeatedly to describe her feelings after her devastating Olympic "loss", Michelle simply stated, "I didn't lose the gold. I won the silver." With quiet confidence, Michelle proclaimed her experience as victory, herself as victor. She did not allow others to define her Olympic experience, or label her as anything less than a champion. In your pursuit of purpose, you will constantly be faced with the definitions, labels, and interpretations of others. To succeed, you must hold fast to your own identity as a champion, and define success for yourself in all circumstances. Learn to see and celebrate your victories in all situations. Know that you are designed for destiny, and insulate your identity from the assault of skeptics, cynics, critics, and commentators. See your triumph in trial. Declare your destiny through delay. See the summit regardless of setbacks. Do not let other people tell you who you are. In all things, you are a champion!

"So, what do you think? With God on our side like this, how can we lose?"

Romans 8:31 (The Message)

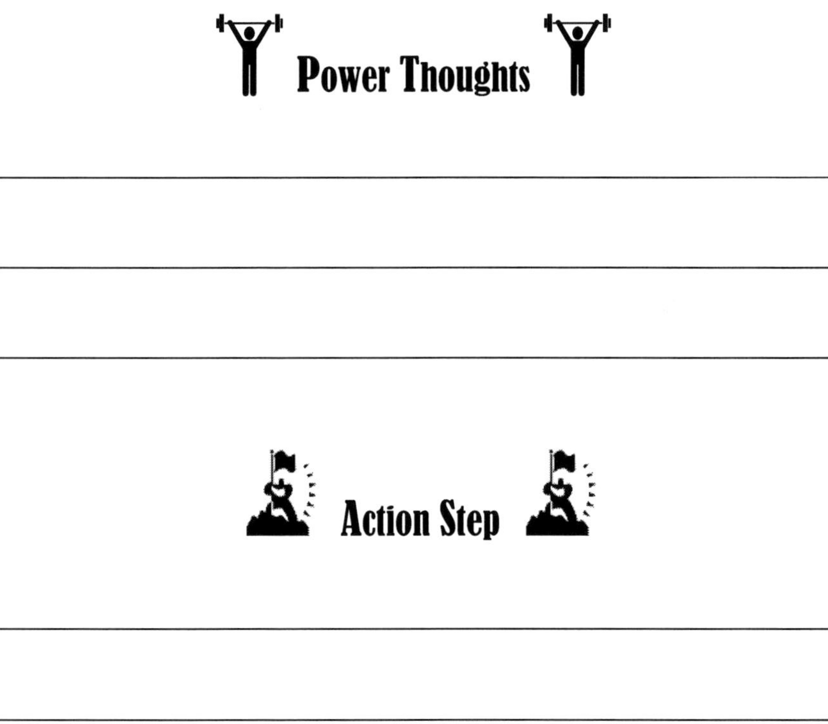

DAY 28 | A.M.

BE TRUE TO YOU

"I prefer to be true to myself, even at the hazard of incurring the ridicule of others, rather than to be false, and to incur my own abhorrence."

–Frederick Douglass, former slave, abolitionist, and my personal hero

Determine in your heart, you will be true to you, no matter the cost. When I was in high school, I played the flute. I studied classical music, and I was exceptionally gifted. Unfortunately, I was teased mercilessly by many of the other black students in my school. Why was I so different? I loved playing the flute so in spite of it, I kept at it. In my senior year, I won national recognition for my scholastic and musical accomplishments. The scholarship offers came in. The crowning moment was when I was recognized by the NAACP for my achievements. Overnight, after years of rejection and ridicule, the NAACP award changed the perceptions of me from traitor to trailblazer. All was forgiven, and new friendships were born. My self-perception didn't change! In spite of being misunderstood, I was always true to myself. If I had crumbled under the criticism, I would have given up my gifting and my goals. The discipline I learned playing the flute I carry to this day. The perfection I experienced in my best performances pushes me to raise my personal best even now. After graduating from college, I remember being invited to play a classical piece at the Martin Luther King, Jr. celebration at Kirtland Air Force Base, New Mexico. I stood before the audience, remembering the torments of high school, yet determined to bring honor to the gift I had been given. After playing for 1,500 people, I received a thunderous standing ovation from a sea of beautiful black faces. Gifted educator and trailblazer Marva Collins said, "Trust yourself. Think for yourself. Act for yourself. Speak for yourself. Be yourself. Imitation is suicide." Amen. Be true to you.

In his grace, God has given us different gifts for doing certain things well…

Romans 12:6 (NLT)

____

____

____

DAY 28 | P.M.

MAKE YOUR MASTERPIECE

"If you hear a voice within you say,
"You cannot paint," then by all means paint,
and that voice will be silenced."
–Vincent Van Gogh

Do you want to silence the *"I can't"* in your life? Step out to do the thing that you are not sure you can do. Start. Set your mind to begin. Action is the antidote for doubt, and the answer to uncertainty. By beginning to create, you will cure your hesitancy and timidity. By doing, you will discover your talents and find your skills. As you practice and hone your skills, you will grow into your strengths. When you stand in your strengths, you will unlock your potential. When your potential is released, you will ultimately mold your masterpiece. At the start, you will rarely see any glimpse of the masterpiece in the making. It is obscured in the humble beginnings of trial and error; masked in mistakes and missteps. In the early stages of starting something new, you must see beyond your first fragile attempts, and envision the future of magnificence with imagination and determination. It is at this delicate time of seeing the future by faith alone that you will often hear the haunting indictment: *"I can't. I can't do it."* Yes you can. Not perfectly, not flawlessly, but rest assured, you can. Step out. Begin. As you continue with determination, your abilities will appear, your expertise will emerge, and your mastery will be magnified. Paint the picture of potential fully realized on the canvas of your life. Silence *"I can't."* Push forward and persevere. Make your masterpiece.

There has never been the slightest doubt in my mind that the God who started this great work in you would keep at it and bring it to a flourishing finish on the very day Christ Jesus appears.

Philippians 1:6 (The Message)

DAY 29 | A.M.

YOU ARE NOT ALONE

"We are, none of us, all alone in this world. Your brothers are here, too."

–Albert Schweitzer

You are not alone! As you continue to strive for success, you will need the help of others. Don't be afraid to reach out and ask for help! None of us succeeds independently. There are many people who are eager to help you. Reach out to your mentors and advisors. Reach out to your role models. Reach out to your encouragers and supporters. Don't fall into the trap of the Lone Ranger Syndrome. The Lone Ranger was a fun TV show, but it's not a good way to approach your goals! Trying to accomplish your goals by yourself is a major mistake, causing unnecessary frustration, disappointment, and worst of all, the temptation to quit and give up. Going it alone can cost you precious time and money, and it can sabotage even the best of ideas. Create your support system. The people around you by default are not necessarily the ones intended to help you accomplish your goals. Carefully consider your plans and then design the ideal support system you need to succeed! One word of encouragement may be just what you need to maintain your endurance. One concept from your coach can solidify your strategy, opening the floodgates to new business opportunities. One correction from your trusted advisor may save you from making a major mistake. One hug from a faithful friend may give you the strength to sustain your journey. To succeed, build a strong support system! You are not alone!

Plans fail for lack of counsel, but with many advisers they succeed.

Proverbs 15:22 (NIV)

Day 29 | P.M.

I BELIEVE IN YOU

"Surround yourself with people who believe you can."
–Dan Zadra

The people that you invite to speak into your life will have an enormous impact on your destiny. Choose wisely! Consciously choose to surround yourself with those who can see beyond your past. Surround yourself with those who can see you overcoming your current circumstances. Surround yourself with those special people who have visionary eyesight; who see where you are going through eyes of faith and belief. Surround yourself with those who will give you unending encouragement and relentless support. Surround yourself with people who believe you can! I am one who commends your climb! I recognize your resilience and applaud your ascent. I believe you can accomplish your goals. I believe you are determined to finish your race. I believe you will rise to fulfill your potential. I am in your corner. I believe in you.

Power Principle

And let us consider and give attentive, continuous care to watching over one another, studying how we may stir up (stimulate and incite) to love and helpful deeds and noble activities, Not forsaking or neglecting to assemble together [as believers], as is the habit of some people, but admonishing (warning, urging, and encouraging) one another, and all the more faithfully as you see the day approaching.

Hebrews 10:24-25 (AMP)

DAY 30 | A.M.

YOU ARE THE ANSWER - BE THE HERO

"I always wondered why somebody doesn't do something about that. Then I realized I was somebody."

–Lily Tomlin

What makes you mad? What gets under your skin? There are certain issues that will stand out to you, and every time you encounter them, your emotions will get triggered. Your sense of justice may rise up, or you may feel a motivating anger. You may feel deep frustration that the issue even exists. These encounters are important indicators of your mission. These triggering events occur when the unique aspects of your personal makeup - your personality, your values, your life experiences, and your gifting - react to the situation at hand, and you are compelled to do something. Your purpose is rising up on the inside. Your passion is being awakened. Solutions may come to mind that seem so obvious, you are astounded no one has taken action yet! Those vital ideas are the answers to the problem, entrusted to you to make them a reality. You are being tapped on the shoulder. You are being selected to lead. You are the one. You alone may hold the key to a different future. You may be the only person that sees the solution. Or, you may be the spark that starts a revolution. Rosa Parks, commenting on her historic decision that marked the beginning of the Civil Rights Movement, said, "I knew someone had to take the first step, and I made up my mind not to move." Take your stand. Implement your ideas. Start the organization. Champion your cause. You are the answer. Be the hero.

Power Principle

Moses answered God, "But why me? What makes you think that I could ever go to Pharaoh and lead the children of Israel out of Egypt?" "I'll be with you," God said. "And this will be the proof that I am the one who sent you: When you have brought my people out of Egypt, you will worship God right here at this very mountain."

Exodus 3:11-12 (The Message)

Power Thoughts

Action Step

DAY 30 | P.M.

CELEBRATE YOUR SUCCESS!

"Realize how good you really are."
–Og Mandino

Do you realize how great you truly are? Take a moment to recognize you are a success! You are an overcomer. You are committed to your goals. You are more than a conqueror. You rise above situations and circumstances. You are determined and dedicated. You don't allow barriers to stand in your way. Thirty days ago, you set a goal to transform your mindset, and you completed it. Take a few minutes to celebrate your success! Learn to stop and celebrate your victories in little things. To achieve success is one thing; to enjoy it is another altogether. Acknowledge your accomplishments! Be comfortable patting yourself on the back and saying, *"Well done!"* When the challenges arise, the words of encouragement that you have spoken to yourself will rise within you. *"I am a great parent. I can handle this!" "I am brilliant in business. I can solve this challenge!"* When you realize how good you really are, you can overcome anything. I celebrate with you. I recognize your greatness. I commend your commitment. Now, celebrate your success!

Power Principle

Therefore, if anyone is in Christ, he is a new creation; old things have passed away; behold, all things have become new.

2 Corinthians 5:17 (NKJV)

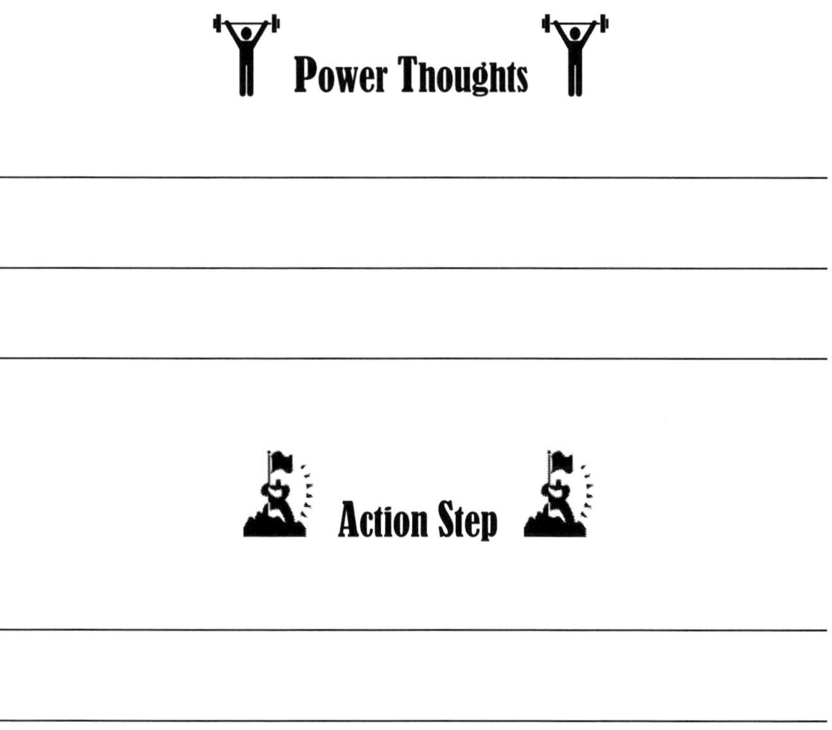

FINAL THOUGHTS

BOLDLY BELIEVE IN YOUR OWN POTENTIAL

"Your willingness to create a new dream or vision for your life is a statement of belief in your own potential."

–David McNally

Do you believe in your own potential for greatness? Do you believe you were purposefully created to do something extraordinary with your life? When you truly recognize your own exquisite design, exponential power, and exceptional magnificence, you will dare to create a vision for your life that is big enough, bold enough, and broad enough to encompass the enormity of your potential. Create a vision that enables you to make your mark. Do not settle for normality. When you believe beyond all doubt that you are destined for the extraordinary, you will ignite the purpose, passion, and perseverance required to bring forth the loving family, the financial independence, the rich relationships, the rewarding work, and the health and vitality you were born to enjoy. Boldly believe in your own potential!

KEEP MOVING

"Life is like a taxi. The meter just keeps a-ticking whether you are getting somewhere or just standing still."

–Lou Erickson

Are you moving forward? Are you building or just busy? Being busy is a deception that masks the truth of our real progress toward our goals, and can lull us into passive acceptance of the status quo, year after year. Did you take a real step forward today? Did you make the phone call, do the workout, sign up for the class, forgive the offense, or plan the family day? Are you keeping track of your progress? Are you measuring your milestones? Experience success in 24-hour victories. Ask yourself each day, "Did I take a real step forward?" Break the busy bubble. Keep moving!

COMMIT AND DO NOT QUIT

"You must have long-range goals to keep you from being frustrated by short-range failures."

–Charles C. Noble

Setbacks happen to all of us. You will have times when you stumble, and unforeseen circumstances will arise to challenge you. During these times, you must keep the bigger picture in mind. Focus on your purpose, and determine to press on despite the turbulence of the present day. A strategy may fail, but you are never a failure. A plan may give way, but you must never give up. Fortify your commitment to your destiny, knowing your purpose is sure. The setbacks of today are stepping stones to future victory if you commit and do not quit!

NEXT STEPS

KEEP INVESTING IN YOURSELF

"Still I am learning."

–Michelangelo

Are you still striving to learn? A 2008 study by the United States Census Bureau found that only 54.3 percent of adults have read any kind of a book, fiction or nonfiction, which was not required for work or school. Other studies have shown that 1/3 of high school graduates never read another book for the rest of their lives; 42 percent of college graduates never read another book after college; and 57 percent of new books are not read to completion. Make the commitment to continue to learn! Do not allow your mind to stagnate, or your goals to be stifled. Make the investment in yourself to continue to read, explore, and grow. Be a life-long learner. Continue to invest in books, classes, seminars, and information products that will help you reach your goals. Stretch yourself to strengthen your skills. Challenge your mind to conquer new concepts. Keep investing in your vision, and your goals will surely come to pass. Keep investing in yourself!

A Special Encouragement If You Are Struggling

MORNING IS COMING!

"It gets dark sometimes,
but morning comes…keep hope alive."
–Jesse Jackson

Are you in a dark season of your life? Morning is coming! Are you facing a situation that looks impossible? Hold on to your hope! In Psalm 30:5, the Bible says, "Weeping may last through the night, but joy comes with the morning." In your quest to climb higher, in some seasons you will soar, and in others, you will struggle. You may go through hard times, but never give up. Devastating circumstances may come against you, but never give up. Your situation will turn for the better if you hold on with tenacity to your hope and faith. Maintain your strong confidence, and never give up. Now is the time to believe and stand strong. Stand your ground. Having done all that you can, just keep standing. Morning is coming. Expect to find the solution to the challenge. Your answer is on the way. If you persevere and do not lose hope, you will make it through your most difficult times. Set your mind to press through it. Be encouraged. A new season is coming. Your joy is coming back. Your peace is coming back. Your strength is coming back. The turning point is coming. You will overcome. Morning is coming!

Psalm 30

1 I will exalt you, LORD, for you rescued me.
You refused to let my enemies triumph over me.
2 O LORD my God, I cried to you for help,
and you restored my health.
3 You brought me up from the grave, O LORD.
You kept me from falling into the pit of death.
4 Sing to the LORD, all you godly ones!
Praise his holy name.
5 For his anger lasts only a moment,
but his favor lasts a lifetime!
Weeping may last through the night,
but joy comes with the morning.
6 When I was prosperous, I said,
"Nothing can stop me now!"
7 Your favor, O LORD, made me as secure as a mountain.
Then you turned away from me, and I was shattered.
8 I cried out to you, O LORD.
I begged the Lord for mercy, saying,
9 "What will you gain if I die,
if I sink into the grave?
Can my dust praise you?
Can it tell of your faithfulness?
10 Hear me, LORD, and have mercy on me.
Help me, O LORD."
11 You have turned my mourning into joyful dancing.
You have taken away my clothes of mourning and clothed me with joy,
12 that I might sing praises to you and not be silent.
O LORD my God, I will give you thanks forever!

Psalm 30 (NLT)

I AM COMMITTED TO YOUR SUCCESS

Thank you for the opportunity to share the wisdom and insights I have gained through my life, my studies, and my Power Coaching™ practice with you. I encourage you to put everything you have learned to work right away in your life. I am committed to your success and passionate about helping you break through barriers and achieve power results fast!

I look forward to connecting with you. Please feel free to email me at **info@madelinealexander.com** to share your experience with reading this book. I personally read each email message, and I look forward to hearing your success stories!

Zig Ziglar said, "People often say that motivation doesn't last. Well, neither does bathing - that's why we recommend it daily." Let's keep your motivation going! I write *Today's Power Tip for Success* every weekday, so please visit **www.madelinealexander.com** to join my subscriber list. I look forward to writing to you each day, helping you stay motivated and moving forward!

For more information on how to Power Coach™ directly with me, visit **www.madelinealexander.com** to learn about Power Coaching for Business™, Power Coaching™ for Individuals, or The Power Coach™ Audio CD Program.

To book a speaking event for your company, organization, university, college, youth organization, or faith-based organization, please email **info@madelinealexander.com**.

YOU CAN ALSO WRITE TO ME AT:

Madeline Alexander, The Power Coach™
Madeline Alexander International
P.O. Box 3109, #19295
Houston, TX 77253-3109

info@madelinealexander.com

I WISH YOU GREAT SUCCESS!

KEEP CLIMBING!

YOU ARE MORE THAN A CONQUEROR!

ABOUT THE AUTHOR

Madeline Alexander, The Power Coach™, is America's premier rapid results success coach and leading authority on lasting breakthrough experiences. Inventor of the revolutionary Power Coaching System™, Madeline specializes in exposing and removing the barriers that are stopping you, your team, or your business organization from taking action and achieving extraordinary results. Madeline delivers dynamic keynotes and transformational seminars for businesses, corporations, colleges and universities, and youth organizations nationwide. Her no-nonsense, truth-telling style, contagious passion and energy, personal transparency, and laser-focused Power Coaching™ techniques will help you cut to the core of your real issues and produce power results in the shortest possible period of time. Madeline resides in Houston, Texas.

POWER COACHING™ GETS RESULTS!

BOOK A SPEAKING ENGAGEMENT:

Madeline Alexander is the ideal speaker for your next conference, seminar, meeting, or event! Email **info@madelinealexander.com** or call **(832) 598-2234** with your event details. Madeline delivers dynamic keynotes and transformational seminars for businesses, corporations, colleges and universities, youth organizations, and faith-based organizations.

POWER COACH™ WITH MADELINE:

Power Coaching for Business™ is the ultimate program for executives, entrepreneurs, corporate leaders, and team managers seeking explosive results. Power Coaching for Individuals™ is best suited for highly motivated individuals who are serious about taking their lives to a whole new level. Visit **www.madelinealexander.com**, email **info@madelinealexander.com**, or call **(832) 598-2234** to request an application, program outline, and suite of services.

ENRICH YOUR GROWTH WITH AUDIO RESOURCES:

The Power Coach™ Audio CD Programs will help you break through barriers, and accelerate your success!
Visit **www.madelinealexander.com** or **www.thepowercoach.com**.

CONNECT ONLINE:

Visit **www.madelinealexander.com** and **www.thepowercoach.com**.
Become Friends at **www.facebook.com/madelinealexander**.
Become a Fan at **www.facebook.com/thepowercoach**.
Follow Madeline at **www.twitter.com/thepowercoach**.
Connect at **www.linkedin.com/in/madelinealexander**.
Email **info@madelinealexander.com**.

www.madelinealexander.com